Firth of Forth

S

NORTHUMBRIA

BERNICIA

Lindisfarne

Bamborough

North Sea

Hexham

Carlisle

Durham

CLYDE

OF N

Jarrow

Weormouth

Whitby

DEIRA

Ripon

Ouse

York

OF ESEY

Humber

Trent

Lincoln

The Wash

Chester

or

Derby

Nottingham

EAST ANGLIA

Tamworth

Leicester

Crowland

Ely

Thetford

Offa's Dyke

Severn

MERCIA

Worcester

Huntington

Bedford

WALES

Gloucester

Colchester

Oxford

Dorchester

ESSEX

London

ISLE OF THANET

Llandaff

Thames

Canterbury

Dover

Glastonbury

Winchester

KENT

Hastings

Strait of Dover

WESSEX

SUSSEX

Exeter

ISLE OF WIGHT

English Channel

THE GOLDEN DRAGON

THE GOLDEN DRAGON

ALFRED THE GREAT AND HIS TIMES

ALF J. MAPP JR.

OPEN COURT   LA SALLE, ILLINOIS

Books by Alf J. Mapp, Jr.

The Virginia Experiment:
The Old Dominion's Role in the Making of America

Frock Coats and Epaulets

America Creates Its Own Literature

Just One Man

The Golden Dragon:
Alfred the Great and His Times

Mapp, Alf Johnson.
 The golden dragon.

 Bibliography: p.
 .1. Alfred the Great, King of England, 840-901. 2. Great Britain—History—Alfred, 871-901. I. Title. DA 153.M25 942.01'64'0924 [B] 74-8983
 ISBN 0-87548-293-7

75-7778

To my wife Ramona Hartley Mapp

CONTENTS

ACKNOWLEDGMENTS

anyone who writes a biography of Alfred the Great owes a debt, whether acknowledged or not, to Asser, the Welsh priest who was the king's Latin teacher and the first chronicler of his life, to the anonymous authors of the *Anglo-Saxon Chronicle,* and to four twentieth century scholars whose contributions to our knowledge of the first Englishmen are incalculable—Sir Frank Stenton, R. H. Hodgkin, Dorothy Whitelock, and Peter Hunter Blair.

Elsewhere in this volume my indebtedness to numerous others who have written about Alfred and his times is acknowledged at appropriate places in the narrative. I have searched the writings of eleven centuries in four languages, drawing light from many sources to illuminate the king and the scene of his labors.

Very direct personal appreciation is due two colleagues at Old Dominion University, Professor Guy T. Holladay of the Department of Foreign Languages, for help in translating difficult passages of German, and Professor David L. Shores, of the English Department, whose expertise in Old English made his services as a proofreader particularly valuable. I am grateful also to two members of the staff of the Hughes Library of Old Dominion University, Professor Benjamin F. Clymer, head of the reference department, and his assistant Rebecca M. Tabakin, interlibrary loan librarian, for their resourcefulness and indefatigable efforts in obtaining research materials. Special thanks go to Professor F. Anne Payne, of the State University of New York at Buffalo, one of the greatest living authorities on the writings of Alfred, whose proofreading was as valuable as her corroborative judgment on many points was reassuring.

On the publication of this, my fifth book, retrospection also compels other acknowledgments: to my mother, Lorraine Carney Mapp, who first taught me how the English language could sing; to my maternal grandmother, Irene Dunaway Carney, who awakened the creative impulse in me and was my first amanuensis; to my father, Alf Johnson Mapp, my first and most helpful critic, a direct descendant of Alfred, who like his famous ancestor, served education with imagination and wit, was resourceful in large things and small, could write an essay or plan a building with equal facility, and met life with courage and candor. Grateful remembrance, too, sheds a special luster on the late Douglas Southall Freeman, often called America's greatest biographer, who encouraged me to write my first book.

But one person, above all, deserves thanks for help with *The Golden Dragon*, as in so many things. My wife, Ramona Hartley Mapp, first suggested that I write a book about Alfred the Great, a character who had intrigued me since childhood. She typed and proofread the manuscript. A former teacher of English at Old Dominion University and at Tidewater Community College, Portsmouth, Virginia, and now chairman of the Division of Humanities and Social Sciences at the latter institution, she provided an informed critical judgment as well as a generously appreciative audience for the testing of alternatives at every stage of my writing. In walks through the woods at our country place on the Corotoman River, in earnest conversations in the study of our Portsmouth home, and by the glow of a log fire while I sought to reproduce the play of firelight on the walls of a Saxon palace, she shared the trials and the joys of my creation. It is simple justice, as well as my great privilege, that this book should be dedicated to her.

ALF J. MAPP JR.
Portsmouth, Virginia
April 19, 1974

THE GOLDEN DRAGON

I

"SO EMINENT
A CANDLESTICK..."

*t*he English are more polite than many nations in the informal titles which they bestow on their rulers. Russia has had its Ivan the Terrible, Germany its Charles the Fat. France has distinguished among four bearers of the name Louis by denominating them the Stammerer, the Spider, the Gross, and the Do-Nothing, and has kept four Charleses straight by calling them the Bad, the Mad, the Bald, and the Simple. Though England has at times been ruled by the mad, the bad, and the gross, her people usually have refrained from fixing insulting appellations on their sovereigns. But, if the English have been sparing in applying pejoratives to royalty, they have been equally restrained in bestowing the highest accolades. Only one of their kings has been called the Great. Alfred is the sole bearer of this title in eleven centuries of English royalty.

Of course, he is the most remarkable sovereign in English, perhaps world, history. That one small nation should produce in a single generation a savior of civilization from barbarian conquest, the father of the burh system of national defense, the greatest naval ar-

chitect in Europe, the creator of a distinctive style of
public architecture, the promulgator of a famous code
of laws, the founder of the oldest continuous literary
tradition in the occident, the originator of a system of
public education, and the producer of translations
from the classics that have endured a thousand years,
is ample reason for pride. But that all these accomplishments should be the work of one man is cause
for astonishment.

And so, not strangely, Alfred has been titled great
by popular consent and scholarly consensus through
many cultural mutations with corresponding changes
of fashion in heroes.[1] Adulation was to be expected
from the authors of the *Anglo-Saxon Chronicle* who
wrote in Alfred's reign and when his son sat upon the
throne. It was to be expected, too, from Asser,[2] who
had been Alfred's friend and the beneficiary of his
largesse, besides being one whose greatest claim to
prestige was his association with Alfred. One might
even say that Ethelweard, in the tenth century, was influenced by the fact that Alfred's blood flowed in his
veins when he called his famous ancestor "that im-
movable pillar of the West Saxons, that man full of
justice, bold in arms, learned in speech, and, above all
things, imbued with divine instruction."[3] But these
words are but the leitmotif of a chorus that has
swelled through the centuries.

The scholar called Florence of Worcester, in the
twelfth century, exercised some restraint in describing
Alfred as "dear to his own race,"[4] but his contemporary, Henry of Huntingdon, apostrophized Alfred:
"Thy toil has given thee lasting reputation....Through all earth's climes none but thyself
e'er lived with power to breathe 'neath such calamities."[5]

By the seventeenth century, Sir John Spelman was
describing the Saxon king as "a Man beyond the
hopes of emulation....Becoming now a light of more
than ordinary splendour, and placed upon so eminent
a Candlestick as a Throne is, there was no Place in
Christendom that received not the glory of his
beams."[6]

4

In the eighteenth century Edward Gibbon called him "the greatest of English kings," and wrote, "Amidst the deepest darkness of barbarism, the virtues of an Antoninus [Marcus Aurelius], the learning and valour of a Caesar, and the legislative spirit of a Lycurgus, were manifested in this patriotic king."[7] So the great English expositor of Roman history saw Alfred as equal to a combination of three of the greatest Romans! And another great historian, David Hume, skeptic philosopher, wrote: "The merit of this prince, both in private and public life, may with advantage be set in opposition to that of any monarch, or citizen, which the annals of any age, or any nation, can present to us. He seems, indeed, to be the model of that perfect character which, under the denomination of a sage or wise man, philosophers have been fond of delineating, rather as a fiction of their imagination than in hopes of ever seeing it really existing."[8]

Even more surprising is the enthusiasm of another eighteenth century skeptic philosopher and historian, Voltaire. Not only did the Frenchman see Alfred's and Charlemagne's courts as the only oases amid the "savage ignorance"[9] of medieval times, but he reserved for the English king a tribute even greater than that which he paid to Louis XIV and Henri IV. Of Alfred he wrote: "I know not whether there has ever been a man on earth worthier of posterity's respect."[10]

Historians of the nineteenth century vied with each other in praising the ninth century king. John Richard Green declared: "The love which he won a thousand years ago has lingered round his name from that day to this. While every other name of those earlier times has all but faded from the recollection of Englishmen, that of Alfred remains familiar to every English child."[11]

Edward A. Freeman, in his monumental *History of the Norman Conquest*, exceeded even this praise to such an extent that Alfred would have been acutely embarrassed if he could have read the words. Calling him "the most perfect character in history," Freeman elaborated:

5

He is a singular instance of a prince who has become a hero of romance, who, as a hero of romance, has had countless imaginary exploits and imaginary institutions attributed to him, but to whose character romance has done no more than justice, and who appears in exactly the same light in history and in fable. No other man on record has ever so thoroughly united all the virtues both of the ruler and the private man. In no other man on record were so many virtues disfigured by so little alloy.[12]

The twentieth century has not been given to unbridled adulation, but, in what has sometimes been called the age of the nonhero, the distinguished historian R. H. Hodgkin has written, "Alfred...displayed the faculty which we call genius. This was exhibited in four ways: in the building of a fleet to deal with the Vikings; in the organizing of a network of fortified burhs; in the development of English literary prose; and in his pioneering interest in the geography of Northern Europe. Any one of these new departures is enough in itself to place Alfred in the front rank of the men who contributed to the progress of the age; taken together they show that he possessed something which can be better described as genius than capacity."[13]

And in this same century Alfred was appraised by one who, like him, was the leader of a beleaguered island people, war chief and peacemaker, writer and historian. Sir Winston Churchill wrote:

Alfred had well defended the Island home. He had by policy and arms preserved the Christian civilization in England. He had built up the strength of that mighty South which has ever since sustained much of the weight of Britain, and later of her Empire. He had liberated London, and happily he left behind him descendants who, for several generations..., carried his work forward with valor and success.[14]

In the 1964 edition of *The Cambridge Medieval History* William John Corbett assessed Alfred as "one of the most remarkable characters known to history."[15]

The verdict is nearly unanimous. Alfred was the Solon, the Hecataeus, the Themistocles, and the Pericles of his people. While it certainly can never be said that we are all Anglo-Saxons in the sense that it is said that "we are all Greeks," it must be admitted that the culture of the English-speaking peoples has had a significant influence since the seventeenth century on the entire Western world and since the eighteenth century on the East as well. The preservation and development of vital elements of that culture, now the heritage of many peoples, was in large part the work of Alfred.

When Alfred became king in his twenty-second year, the light of civilization flickered dimly in his tiny island kingdom on the perimeter of a Western European culture menaced by the rival Saracens on the south and east and overrun by the barbaric Vikings in the north and west.

Amid the howling gales from the North, that small flame guttered low on the rim of darkness. But the young ruler, at times more fugitive than monarch, guarded and fed it so well that it flared forth from its Saxon headland not only as a light to many lands in his own generation but as a beacon across the cluttered sweep of eleven centuries to our own time. Small wonder that historians, through all the controversies of vision and revision that have made revered memorials into dishonored effigies, have consistently united in echoing the popular verdict that Alfred was indeed great. Nor is it beyond the range of possibility, since the survival and growth of civilization have proved to be a matter of challenge and response, that future generations will find it profitable to study the career of Alfred, finding in the microcosm of his life and times lessons applicable to the macrocosmic crises of their own.

7

II

BATTLE OF DRAGONS

the sea dragons kept coming, running up the rivers deep into the land. Where foliage along the banks obscured all below the proudly arched necks, these fearsome creatures seemed to glide through the fields like slithering amphibians, their hideously beautiful red and blue heads lunging forward in ominous surveillance of the countryside.

In the ninth century the Viking dragons followed the whale paths across the northern seas to the British Isles, sailed up the rivers of Russia, raided the empire of Charlemagne. The bold red and white stripes of their sails bellied audaciously against the blue of the Mediterranean. Today we know little more about the forces impelling this restless movement from Scandinavia than did the Europeans of the Dark Ages who prayed, "O Lord, from the fury of the Northmen deliver us." Some historians have suggested that problems of overpopulation in a polygamous society coincided with the attainment of shipbuilding skills surpassing any marine carpentry the world had hitherto known. Whatever the cause, the dragons struck again and again at the coasts of Europe, destroying

9

the Irish monasteries and the learning which they fostered, occupying as their own lands in Britain and
along the Baltic. Contemptuous of the culture of
Western Christendom but masters of its crafts and
matchless in the arts of war, the Vikings seemed as in-
vincible as they were implacable. On Christmas Day,
A.D. 800, Charlemagne, noble in flowing hair and lux-
uriant beard, looking as much like a wise man from
the East as a conqueror of the West, had knelt in the
vast candle-lit interior of St. Peter's in Rome and received from Pope Leo III the crown of the Holy Roman Empire. This latecomer to Roman glory could
stand tall in the procession of the Caesars. He had
welded into one kingdom most of Europe west of the
Elbe. To the south the Mediterranean was his moat
and the Pyrenees and the Alps were his cloud-capped
battlements. The whole Romano-German world paid
him homage—except for the Anglo-Saxons in their
white-cliffed island and the Scandinavians in the pen-
insula of the long night. Yet Charlemagne would one
day stand in impotent rage, the muscles of his neck
bulging like whipcords as through uncontrollable tears
he watched the dragon heads prowling along his Mediterranean shore.[1] And at Christmas, on the fifty-sixth
anniversary of Charlemagne's Roman coronation, the
Northmen would sack Paris, returning later to exact
tribute from his heirs. The 270 miles that lay between
the Frankish monastery of Luxeil and the sea were
not enough to save it from engulfment by the Norse
tide. One Viking chieftain, Thorgestr, installed his
gold-braceleted wife, Ota, as high priestess before the
altar of God in Clonmacnoise, Ireland's most holy
place. The dragon ships, each propelled by forty to
sixty oarsmen, moved up the Rhine and the Elbe with
the same majestic inexorability with which they issued
from their native fiords. Pisa was not far enough
south to escape. And they took the northern land of
the Slavs and gave it the name Russia.

Nowhere did the blue and red dragons meet their
match. Nowhere until, from the little island that like
Scandinavia lay outside the Carolingian Empire, there

stepped forth a golden dragon to confront his gaudy cousins from the North.

The golden dragon was the symbol of the House of Wessex. The great eighteenth century historian Vico, who was also the father of comparative linguistics, found significance in the fact that Draco, or Dragon, was the name given the great law giver of Athens while a dragon was also the symbol of civil power in China. "It is something to wonder at," he observed in *The New Science*, "that two nations so distant in space and time should think and express themselves in the same poetic manner."[2] Vico would have wondered more if he had known that the dragon was also the ensign of the royal house whose greatest representative was the law giver of England. But the laws that Alfred gave the English, as surely though not as literally as those that Draco gave the Athenians, would be manifest only after writing in blood. The golden dragon of the House of Wessex made his appearance two generations before Alfred in pages of history as carmined with blood-red characters as any illuminated manuscript of Saxon lore.

A small splash of blood marks the story's beginning in 787; it is told laconically in the *Anglo-Saxon Chronicle* and with additional details by Ethelweard.[3] On a summer's day in that year an observer on a hillock below Dorchester could have descried a party of several horsemen galloping over the chalky downs toward the harbor, their cloaks streaming behind them. In the lead was Beaduherd, the king's reeve. He had been in Dorchester when word came that three strange ships had arrived in the harbor, six miles or so away. Leaping on his horse, he had ridden with several men to meet the newcomers. It was his business to meet all strangers landing on these shores. If they were merchants or friendly visitors, he would assure them of protection of the king and provide them with an escort to town. Of course, he must be sure that they were not enemies, but, as he had told his companions in Dorchester, he was confident these were merchants. Arrived at the shore, he saw three dragon-prowed

11

long boats. The men who had sailed them, in their tunics and cross garters, looked much like his countrymen. Still there was something fierce in their demeanor. And so, according to some hidden witness whose report has come down to us through Ethelweard, Beaduherd "addressed them in a commanding tone and ordered them to go to Dorchester." For answer, they killed him and his men. Wessex had met its first Viking raiders.

There was no immediate influx of Northmen, but six summers later they swept down on the neighboring kingdom of Northumbria. "In this year," says the *Chronicle*, "dire portents appeared over Northumbria and sorely frightened the people. They consisted of immense whirlwinds and flashes of lightning, and fiery dragons were seen flying in the air. A great famine immediately followed those signs, and a little after that in the same year, on 8 June, the ravages of heathen men miserably destroyed God's church on Lindisfarne, with plunder and slaughter."[4] Whatever the origin of the fiery dragons in the air, the identity of the fire-bearing dragons that came by sea is certain. They were Vikings. When Alcuin of York, then the foremost scholar at Charlemagne's court, learned what had befallen his old homeland, he lamented:

"For almost 350 years, we and our fathers have dwelt in this fair land, and never before have such terrors appeared in Britain like these...and it was not thought possible that such havoc could be made."[5]

Next summer the Vikings raided Northumbria again, sacking the monastery of Jarrow at the mouth of the River Don. But one of their leaders was killed and, as almost eight centuries later with another invading armada, some of the enemy's ships were broken by a fierce storm. Many of the sailors drowned. Those who reached the shore alive were instantly killed.[6]

Not till 835 did the Vikings return. Then in 836 they arrived in force. The crews of thirty-five ships, each propelled by thirty-two oars, poured ashore at Carhampton. King Egbert, Alfred's grandfather, took a heavy toll of the enemy, but many of his own men were lost, including two bishops and two earls,[7] and at the end of the day the Danes had possession of the field. Two years later a seemingly greater force of ships landed in Cornwall, won the West Welsh as allies, and in combined strength moved against the West Saxons. Egbert met the two armies at Hingston Down and defeated both.[8]

But raids came with the regularity of the seasons. In 842, the largest town in the island, London, in neighboring Mercia, was one of those communities sacked with great slaughter.[9] Eventually not a Saxon church remained within a day's ride of the sea.

The loss to scholarship and commerce was almost incalculable. But the mass of Saxons saw the Viking raids in more personal terms. The Northmen, like fearsome beasts in their horned helmets, would suddenly sweep down on a farm or village, slaying the menfolk. Sometimes they would separate their victim's ribs from his breastbone, spreading them out in hideous imitation of the raven that was their battle emblem. Sometimes he would be left to die slowly within the aura of heat from his burning dwelling, the last image of his fading vision the sight of his wife or daughter spraddled on the ground with her tunic around her neck and her linen underwear in shreds, struggling futilely with a Viking warrior whose rough breastplate bit into her white flesh.[10]

Among the proverbs of the Northmen was no such tame admonition as "the early bird gets the worm." Their young men actually were told, "the early man takes another's wealth—or his life."[11] Violence and rapine were not departures from Norse codes of conduct; they were the expressions of avowed ideals.

Alfred's grandfather Egbert's defeat of the Danes and their West Welsh allies in 837 was the greatest in a series of personal triumphs that made Wessex the island's foremost kingdom and its strongest obstruction to Viking conquest.[12] Egbert came to the throne in 802 from exile. So long as Beorthric wore the crown of Wessex with the blessings of his overlord, the king

of Mercia, Egbert could not safely return to his homeland. Though his father had been only a sub-king in
Kent, the blood of Wessex's ancient rulers flowed in
his veins and perhaps it was thought that some of
their enterprise animated him. In any event, the years
of exile proved a blessing for him and his country, for
he stayed at the court of Charlemagne, learning the
arts of government and war from the most powerful
ruler in Christendom. When Beorthric's death made
Egbert's return possible, he quickly established his
claim to the throne. In the first thirteen years of his
reign, his acquiescence in Mercian overlordship gave
little indication of how well he had learned his lessons
from the emperor of the Holy Roman Empire. In the
next five years, the fruits of his study were dramatically revealed. In August of 825 he challenged Mercian domination and defeated his overlord, King
Beornwulf, in the Battle of Ellendun, fought near the
site of the present town of Swindon. Egbert then de-
tached a large force from his army and sent it, under
command of his son Ethelwulf, Bishop Ealhstan of
Sherborne, and Earl Wulfheard, to Kent, where Egbert's father had ruled as sub-king, and they drove
King Bealdred north across the Thames. The people
of Kent, Surrey, Sussex, and Essex flocked to the
standard of the House of Wessex, apparently eager to
acknowledge representatives of the family that had
ruled them in happier days and appealing to Egbert
for protection from the Mercians. Before the year was
out, the Mercian king was killed by the people of East
Anglia—while invading their territory, Florence of
Worcester said.[13] He was succeeded by Ludeca who
was killed in 827 with five of his earls, apparently
when he led an army into East Anglia to avenge
Beornwulf's death. East Anglia now appealed for Egbert's protection, and he added it to his growing empire. As Egbert's *secundarius,* or viceroy, young Ethelwulf ruled the four provinces freed from Mercian
domination.

For the year 827 the superstitious scribes of the *Anglo-Saxon Chronicle* noted an eclipse of the moon on

14

Christmas Eve and recorded in the same paragraph the eclipse of Mercian empire.[14] In that year Egbert conquered Mercia itself and all lands south of the Humber, becoming the eighth man in British history to win the title "bretwalda," ruler of Britain.

But Egbert's empire might yet be challenged from the north. A short while before, Northumbria had been much more powerful than Wessex and a king of Northumbria had once been "bretwalda." Against this last Saxon kingdom independent of his rule, Egbert led an army in 829. He met the Northumbrian leaders at Dore, in what is now North Derbyshire, and, in the words of the *Chronicle*, "they offered him submission and peace there, and on that they separated."[15]

The next year Wiglaf, whom Egbert had deposed as king of Mercia, regained the throne. Egbert was busy fighting the Welsh, whom he "reduced...to humble submission."[16] Perhaps Wales was not then a reasonable exchange for Mercia, but Egbert might well congratulate himself on having moved from the base of a tiny subordinate kingdom to destroy one empire and build another—all within the space of five years.

As we have seen, he was not to enjoy this empire in peace. The Vikings sacked Sheppey in 835, one year before defeating Egbert at Carhampton. And, of course, in 838 he was forced to fight the Vikings in combination with the West Welsh. The victory that he won over them at Hingston Down was to be his last. He died in 839.

Ethelwulf succeeded his father, and gave to his own son Athelstan the government of those kingdoms and provinces which Ethelwulf himself had once governed as viceroy for Egbert.

As a youthful military commander and as his father's viceroy, Ethelwulf had proved his ability. Few of his subjects could have doubted his capacity. But did he have the fierce drive with which Egbert had lifted himself to imperial rank? A vast reservoir of disciplined energy would be needed—perhaps to fend off rebellion, certainly to throw back the Viking attacks. Some must have remembered that Egbert had reigned for thirteen years before revealing the energetic will that changed the history of five kingdoms in as many years. But it seemed unlikely that Ethelwulf would be granted thirteen years in which to focus his energies. In 840 the crews of thirty-three Viking ships poured ashore at Southampton and in the same year a Danish army ravaged Dorset. One of Ethelwulf's earls, Wulfheard, defeated the Vikings at Southampton. Another earl, Ethelhelm, put the Danes to flight at Portland, but the tide of battle turned and the invaders won the field, killing Ethelhelm. Before the end of the year Wulfheard died. Ethelwulf still could rely on the stout fighting qualities of a few remaining earls. But there was one less after 841 when Hereberht was slain in Romney Marsh by Vikings who scourged East Anglia and Kent. The next year Viking torches and swords made a path through London and left much of Rochester in ruins.[17] A king was not compelled by honor to be in the forefront of battle, but Egbert at his height would not have been satisfied to leave the field command to others.

Ethelwulf must have been stirred by memories of his father when in 843 he learned that thirty-five ships of the enemy had arrived at Carhampton. This was precisely the message, even to the exact number of ships, that Egbert had received seven years before. Egbert then had led the fight against the Danes and lost. His son now seized the initiative and also met defeat. At least, though, Ethelwulf *had* seized the initiative. Perhaps he would yet fight his own battle of Hingston Down.

But, in the next great phase of the struggle, others again took the lead. In 845, two earls and a bishop led the people of Somerset and Dorset to victory over the Danish army.

Ethelwulf seemed to perform the routine duties of the kingship with scant sign of the enthusiasm with which he now pursued religious thought or which he brought to relations with his growing family. His sixth child, the fifth son, was born in 849 at Wantage on the Berkshire Downs. He was the first member of the family to be named Alfred.[18]

It seemed unlikely that this prince, fourth from the throne by descent, would ever become a king. Indeed, unless Ethelwulf found a better way to cope with the Viking menace, it was unlikely that any of his sons would wear a crown. For in 851, the Vikings for the first time wintered in England. They were no longer mere raiders; they were determined upon conquest. Astonished Saxons saw 350 dragon-prowed ships in the mouth of the Thames. Canterbury and London were sacked. The king of the Mercians and his army fled south of the Thames into Surrey.[19]

The king of Wessex now showed his mettle. And his sons with him. The eldest, Athelstan, beat back a Viking force in Kent, capturing nine of their ships. With the next son, Ethelbald, at his side, and the men of Wessex at his back, Ethelwulf moved against the main army of the Danes, a force of perhaps 10,000 men. The Viking warriors included the fierce *berserkers*, madmen who flung themselves into the frenzy of battle without thought of death. Behind them were disciplined fighters unexcelled in Europe and with swords superior to those wielded by any other soldiers in the West. But that day they were no match for the erstwhile peaceful Ethelwulf, turned terrible in battle. Afterward, the scribe of the *Anglo-Saxon Chronicle* exulted that the king of Wessex had "inflicted the greatest slaughter on a heathen army that we ever heard tell of."[20]

Ethelwulf's preeminence in the island was recognized two years later when Burgred, king of the Mercians, and his council appealed to the king of Wessex for aid against Wales. Ethelwulf led his army across Mercia to the Welsh and, in the words of the *Chronicle*, "made them all submissive to him."[21] The union with the Mercians was cemented shortly after Easter when Ethelwulf gave his daughter in marriage to King Burgred.[22]

But the threat of Danish conquest still hung over the island like a marrow-chilling fog. The men of Kent and Surrey were battling the Vikings, with heavy losses on both sides. But they fought the harder because their king and his sons were mighty warriors.

THE GOLDEN DRAGON Egbert had made Wessex the chief barrier to Viking conquest. His son had roused from dreams of peace to reassert Saxon defiance in the eleventh hour. Wherever the blue and red dragons struck, Saxon hopes, no less than Saxon soldiers, clustered around the Golden Dragon of Wessex.

III

TEENAGED GENERAL

the dragons most familiar to four-year-old Alfred probably were the slim, long-necked creatures, somewhat like attenuated dinosaurs, whose gracefully entwined tails formed decorative arabesques on various articles of furniture.[1] Of course he also probably saw the Golden Dragon on an ensign that accompanied the royal entourage when it traveled from one of the king's manors to another and on arrival was mounted on a palisade or wall to signalize the presence of the royal family.[2] The small boy did not know that all this traveling made it possible for his father to grant audience to subjects in every part of his realm and to make the royal presence felt everywhere. He did know that there was special excitement when the wagon train left behind the squat stone buildings of Winchester, the principal capital, and headed along the white road over the chalky downs to Dorchester, for there the family celebrated Christmas. There was then generally a nip in the air that made him thankful for the leather hoods of the covered wagons and sometimes there was a cloak of snow, even whiter than the road, that hid both the path and

the neighboring fields. The frostiness of the outer air
made doubly welcome the great hall with its roaring
fire. There was excitement when the Yule log, carcass
of a great oak, was drawn in by men whose straining
legs bulged against their cross-gartered trousers. The
excitement grew as the log was lit with a remnant of
its predecessor from the previous Christmas, seeming
to catch, then wavering so precariously as to cause a
collective holding of breath as if all were afraid to fan
so feeble a spark, finally bursting into a bold flame
that brought cheers that seemed to rise to the rafters
with the shadows that twisted there in obedience to
the leaping fire. Undoubtedly there were gifts in this
happy season that combined pagan rejoicing at winter's death with the engrafted joys of Christian fellow-
ship. An illuminated manuscript indicates that toy
pigs were popular presents, at least with some children.

The trip to Wantage also held excitement for
Alfred. The Berkshire town in the Vale of the White
Horse was his birthplace. The boy must have marveled at the rude grandeur of the gigantic charger,
stark white against the green of the hillside as it had
been since removal of the turf generations before to
reveal the chalk beneath. And, since his father was a
king whose ensign was a golden dragon, Alfred's imagination must have been stimulated by the nearly
bald mound called Pendragon, "chief of dragons" or
"chief of kings" in the old Celtic tongue.

Easter, of course, would have been reverently observed by the religious-minded House of Wessex, particularly under the leadership of Alfred's pious father.
This holiday of rejoicing was central to the ecclesiastical calendar; all the movable feasts were arranged
around it. Easter was frequently spent at Wilton, on
the broad uplands of Wiltshire that reached above the
island mists toward the sun. After Easter the move
was to Chippenham. It was here, near the border of
Mercia, that Alfred's sister, undoubtedly with the
small brother looking on, was married to the new ruler of that kingdom.

Shortly afterward came a break in Alfred's round of insular journeying. His father sent him to Rome. No one now knows why Ethelwulf should have sent his four-year-old son to Rome in the summer of 853 A.D. One historian has suggested that the king felt some member of the house should make a pilgrimage to Rome and selected the boy because "as the youngest member of the royal family, he was regarded as expendable."[3] But this possibility seems unlikely in view of Ethelwulf's reputed kindliness, especially if we accept the testimony of Alfred's friend Asser that the boy "was loved by his father and mother, and indeed by everybody, with a united and immense love, more than all his brothers, and was always brought up in the royal court...."[4] Whatever his reasons for selecting so young an emissary, Ethelwulf doubtless was convinced that he should visit Rome, by proxy at least. In the first year of his reign he vowed to make the journey and had even sought permission to travel through the Kingdom of the Franks, after hearing the direful prophecy of a priest whose words had the fateful ring of Tiresias' speech to Oedipus.

> If Christians do not repent quickly of their crimes and wickednesses, and do not observe the Lord's Day with much more reverence, a great and irresistible disaster will quickly overtake them. For three days and nights a thick cloud will cover the land, and then immediately afterwards the pagans will come with a vast number of ships, and will destroy with fire and sword the land, and the people themselves with all their possessions. Nevertheless, if the people are prepared to repent and abandon their sins by fasting and almsgiving, they may succeed in avoiding all these disasters.[5]

Since then the Danes had come repeatedly in huge fleets to ravage with fire and sword. Of course, Ethelwulf had won a great victory over them in 851, but they still menaced the land. The pilgrimage should not be delayed. Why, then, did Ethelwulf himself not go? Perhaps he feared internal troubles if he remained long out of the country, or thought that he should stay in Wessex to lead his people in repelling

21

an always possible massive attack by the Danes. Or
could superstition have kept him from Rome? Two of
his ancestors had visited the city. Caedwalla, after
bringing Isle of Wight, Sussex, and Kent under Wessex domination, had made a pilgrimage to Rome and
died ten days after baptism there. Ine, a great king of
Wessex, had made his pilgrimage to Rome in 726 and
also had died there.[6] Perhaps it was better that the
journey be made by one who had not yet assumed
even a portion of the duties of leadership.

Superstition aside, the trip was fraught with peril.
From time to time, great Viking fleets swept through
the English Channel. The Kingdom of the Franks—
through which Alfred's course doubtless lay—was beset by Viking raids and inner turmoil. Rome itself
rested none too securely behind untested fortifications
only a year old. It was hard to sprawl at ease beneath
a sun that a few years before had glinted off the scim-
itars of Moors dropping from the walls.

For Alfred the parting from his father and his
mother must have been painful. The king seems to
have been closer to his family than were his counterparts in many kingdoms. And Queen Osburh, described by Asser as "noble both by birth and by
nature,"[7] has come down to subsequent generations
chiefly through a glimpse of her as a mother who enjoyed reading to her children. Undoubtedly the parting from her youngest son was hard for her, but if
she was, as Asser says, "a very devout woman,"[8] she
must have acquiesced with good grace.

Whatever Alfred's apprehensions, he must have
been excited at the prospect of adventures in strange
lands. And in his retinue there surely were faces
hardly less familiar than those of his own family.
Some of the friends accompanying him doubtless
wore the conical helmets and chain mail shirts of the
king's bodyguards. He probably thought that, with
their straight-edged long swords and round wooden
shields covered in oxhide, they would be more than a
match for any enemy encountered.[9] And surely someone must have carried one of those small harps whose

strings the scops plucked as they chanted tales of heroism under the smoky rafters of the mead hall. Much of Alfred's world was going with him on his journey. But still, for a four-year-old child, the parting from his mother and father must have been disturbing.

Probably Alfred's itinerary included Paris. Not only had his father sought permission to travel through the Kingdom of the Franks when he himself had contemplated the journey to Rome, but when he finally made it years later he stopped over at the capital on the Seine.[10] The Saxon prince, not yet having seen the great city on the Tiber, surely marveled at the stone buildings of Paris, however provincial the Frankish capital may have appeared to more sophisticated eyes. It certainly dwarfed Winchester which, except for its modest stone cathedral, a little like a solid country church of later centuries, consisted mostly of timbered dwellings, altogether presenting the appearance of a small market town. And the other towns in Wessex were really villages. Even most of the king's palaces were wooden—huge, high-beamed, drafty farmhouses with double-doored great halls whose ornamental wall-hangings rippled when the wind blew.[11]

More surprises awaited the little boy when they reached the Alps. These snow-capped heights made Pendragon, seat of kings, seem a mere footstool.

Yet none of the wonders prepared Alfred for Rome itself. It was hard to tell which was more remarkable, the massive stolidity of the great stone buildings or the torrential rush of people through the sluices between them. In the Kingdom of the Franks, men had dressed much as they did back in Wessex. But here in Rome the cross garters of the Saxons marked them as aliens even though each wore his cloak, fastened with a jeweled brooch at the shoulder, as proudly as any Roman. The monuments of the city discouraged self-importance. The restorer's hand had not yet reconstructed the fallen glories of the Forum; Alfred and his companions were dwarfed by shattered pillars, lonely remnants of an imperialism that centuries before had counted the fog-wrapped island of the An-

gles and Saxons as its most obscure outpost. There
was the huge-domed Pantheon with its round central
skylight opening upon the still vaster dome of heaven
itself. Here their prayers echoed in an edifice dedicated some eight centuries before to all the gods of the
Romans but now serving as a Christian temple and
the repository of the bones of some three thousand
Christian martyrs. Not far away was the scene of their
martyrdom, the Coliseum where men and women had
walked forth to die for their faith, while tiers of spectators cheered the devouring lions.[12] Alfred must have
wondered if he could be that brave.

Rome considered itself the capital of the civilized
world. It was generally conceded to be the spiritual
capital of Western Christendom. Alfred was to be not
merely a spectator of its pomp, but a participant. His
was no ordinary audience with the pope. For that
matter, this pope was no ordinary man. Leo IV[13] had
assumed office without waiting for imperial endorse-
ment and had so impressed his personality on Rome
that the part of it within his newly constructed walls
was henceforward known as the Leonine City. In the
year of Alfred's birth this pope, finding the secular
leaders of the Italian states cringing before the as-
saulting Saracens and sometimes making deals with
them, led his own naval expedition against the Moors
and put them to flight. The red-robed man who sat
on the papal throne was now engaged in another
campaign and the four-year-old Saxon boy who stood
before him, though the child did not know it, was
about to play a part in the struggle. Leo had let it be
known that he had accepted the office of pope so that
he might assume responsibility for "all that happen[ed] in the world."[14] Indeed, he had said that if he
failed to deal with any situation—secular as well as ecclesiastical—that needed correction, he would have to
answer to God for his failure. Seeing himself as heir
to the Roman emperors as well as to St. Peter, Leo
chose not only to declare Alfred his spiritual son but
also to "gird him with the honor and the outward
trappings...of a consul of Rome."[15] The honor was by

24

no means unique, but it made a deep impression on the boy and his retinue. The *Anglo-Saxon Chronicle* mistakenly declared that Alfred had been "conse-crated...king,"[16] or, in other words, had been accord-ed a spiritual coronation, presumably in preparation for a possible assumption of rule in future years. It is easy to understand why the ceremony was memorable for the boy. He was girded with a sword and invested with a white and purple cloak; finally, a crown was placed upon his head.

How long Alfred remained in Rome we do not know. But his experiences in the great cosmopolitan city doubtless raised his horizons even at his tender age. Not very long after his return to Wessex he dis-covered still another world. This discovery came one day when he was five or six years old. His mother showed him and his brothers a book of Saxon poetry. "I will give this book," she said, "to the one of you who can learn it first."[17] The volume may have been of the sort described by the Saxons as "made splendid with red and gold."[18] Alfred's eye lit upon the bril-liantly illuminated initial letter, which he was to re-member years later as "beautiful." Excitedly, before his older brothers spoke, he asked: "Will you really give that book to the one who can first understand it and say it back to you?" Smiling at his eagerness, she assured him, "Yes, I will." Taking the book before she could hand it to him, Alfred hurried to a teacher at the court. A short while later, he returned with the book, reciting the lines of verse page by page. He had not learned to read, but he had fulfilled his part of the bargain and the book was his. Alfred had become a student of books and a book collector. He would never lose his appetite for these pursuits.

Shortly after this pleasant incident, the queen died. It may well be imagined that Alfred, believed to be her favorite son,[19] missed so devoted and understand-ing a mother. Fortunately, an event soon after her death brought Alfred even closer to his father. Ethel-wulf, perhaps fearing some connection between his wife's death and his neglected vow to visit Rome, or

simply reminded of Death's power to thwart the best
of intentions, set out for Italy with Alfred as his companion.

Alfred's eagerness in pointing out to his father
sights familiar to the boy from his journey two years
before is easy to conceive. In Paris they were entertained at the Frankish court, where Alfred's grandfather had found hospitality in his years of exile. The
host this time was Charles II, king of the West Franks
and grandson of Charlemagne. This Charles, if a
contemporary portrait may be believed, was a long-
faced, mustached, short bearded man, not so impos-
ing in appearance as his grandfather but much trim-
mer figured.[20] The great empire of Charlemagne had
been partitioned among his descendants so that
Charles the Bald, as he came to be called, ruled over
only a fraction of the territory which his grandfather
had dominated. And, at the time of Alfred's visit,
Charles's hold on even this fragment, France, was ten-
uous at best. The Bretons had renounced their allegiance to him and were perpetually on the verge of
an alliance with the Vikings who attacked his coast almost every year. Moreover, he had just been forced to
relinquish direct control of Aquitaine, though he had
succeeded in making his son its king. At the very time
of Ethelwulf and Alfred's visit, a movement toward
revolt was gaining rapidly among the magnates.
Nonetheless, only a naive man would have counted
Charles out at this point. He had much of his grandfather's boldness and resourcefulness and, like him,
dreamed of restoring learning among his subjects.
Charles II would be counted among France's able rulers. He was worth knowing.

In Charles's turbulent kingdom, the escort to the
border that he provided for his guests was most welcome. Indeed, a special escort would have been welcome in Rome itself, for that city at about the time of
Ethelwulf and Alfred's arrival was more strife-torn
than France. Alfred must have been disappointed to
learn that his godfather, Leo IV, who had invested
him with the dignity of a Roman consul, had died in

July. He must have been shocked by the fate of Leo's
successor, Benedict III. Adherents of Anastasius, his
chief rival in the papal elections, tore the new pope's
vestments from him, beat him, and threw him in prison. He was eventually freed by his friends but riotous
Rome was not until fall sufficiently quiet for his consecration.

Ethelwulf and Alfred seem to have arrived in Rome
during some part of this contention, or perhaps just
as a modicum of order had been restored. In any
event, they did not seek the safety of anonymity. Nor
did the ordinary citizens of Rome laugh at the provincial, cross-gartered Saxons come to the capital of civilization. They were too busy scrambling for the silver
coins which Ethelwulf flung to them as he rode
through the streets. They were happy enough to carry
away these miniature "portraits" of the Saxon king.
And the nobles and clergy were delighted with the
gold which he showered upon them. Especially dramatic was the meeting between Ethelwulf and Benedict. If a pope could "crown" a Saxon prince,
investing him with robes and girding him with a
sword, then a Saxon king could be equally generous
to a pope. Ethelwulf brought Benedict a crown of
pure gold, a gold-ornamented sword, and a white silk
dalmatic and alb resplendent with gold and silver
thread. The evidence of Saxon wealth and Saxon artistry must have caused many at the papal court to
reevaluate these travelers from the end of the world.
Papal courtiers must have marveled, too, at the intricacy of design and skill in execution exemplified by
the gold candelabra and silver hanging lamps which
Ethelwulf brought to light the sanctuaries of Rome.
Six centuries later, in a famous fresco, Raphael would
commemorate the visit of the Saxon king.[22]

Alfred and his father remained in the city for a
year or more. What, if any, formal instruction the boy
received there is not known; but the stay in Rome-
burh, as Alfred always called it (even the eternal city
was not exempt from easy Anglicization) was an important part of his education. Its columns and arches

27

would remain his ideal of architecture years later in a
land of timbered palaces. He would remember days in
the English quarter—a community of Saxon ecclesiastics, noblemen, traders, and transients—as well as the
exciting diversity of crowds in the main thorough-
fares—helmeted heads framed by blonde locks,
cowled heads, turbaned heads, all bobbing amid a tur-
bulence of tongues. He would never forget that there
was a great world beyond England's shores. And the
Vatican Court, like the court of Charlemagne that was
still talked of in his family, would be a reminder that
a seat of power could also be a center of learning.

The court of Charlemagne's grandson, Charles the
Bald, was a stopping place on the return from Rome,
just as it had been on the way to Italy. But this time
weeks stretched into months. What amusements
Alfred found we do not know. Charles's young
daughter, Judith, was considered very attractive, but
since she must have been almost fourteen years old, if
not already that age, she may have been too far into
adolescent sophistication to spend much time trying to
entertain a seven-year-old boy. Apparently, she succeeded in entertaining his middle-aged father. Alfred
must have been amazed, if not shocked, to learn that
Judith was going to become his father's wife, that this
young girl would become his own stepmother.

The wedding was on October 1, 856, at Verberie-
sur-Oise, near Compiègne. Alfred, doubtless wonder-
ing what the future held for him, saw her receive an
honor that his own mother had never enjoyed. She
was crowned queen-consort as Hincmar, archbishop
of Rheims and famous scholar, intoned:

> The Lord crown thee with glory and honor and
> place upon thy head the precious stones of the Spirit;
> that the glitter of gold and sparkle of jewels here may
> be a token of the glory which may ever shine forth in
> thee and in thy doings....[23]

She would sit on her own throne at his father's side in
equal dignity with the king himself.

What did Alfred think of this arrangement? Many
years later he let his good friend Asser know that he

considered it an unwise one. It was contrary to West
Saxon custom. Alfred told him why. An earlier king
of Wessex, Beorthric, had married Eadburh, daughter
of the great Mercian king Offa, and had raised her to
equal dignity with himself. According to Asser's report of what Alfred told him, the queen committed so
many crimes "that she not only earned for herself ex-
clusion from the throne, but also brought the same
stigma upon those who came after her; for, because
of the wickedness of that queen, all the nobles...swore together that they would never let any
king rule over them who should attempt to place a
queen on the throne by his side."[24] Asser says that
Alfred told him that Eadburh, whenever she was frus-
trated in getting the king to remove one of his old
friends from power, resorted to poison. King Beorthric's own death, Alfred firmly believed, resulted from
his drinking a poisoned draught which the queen had
prepared for one of his courtiers. Eadburh then fled
to the court of Charlemagne, carrying royal treasures
with her. Standing before the throne, she offered him
money in exchange for protection. Instead of answer-
ing her directly, he said, "Choose, Eadburh, between
me and my son, who stands here with me." The
bearded face of Charlemagne was still kingly but age
had given him a most unmajestic potbelly.[25] "If I am
to have my choice," she said, "I choose your son because he is younger than you." Charlemagne smiled,
but not in a way to warm her heart. "If you had chosen me, you would have had my son, but as you have
chosen him, you shall not have either of us."

But, in the way of tolerant monarchs, believing her
unfit for secular rule, he had her made abbess of a
large convent. A few years later she was convicted of
having "unlawful intercourse with a man of her own
nation" and was expelled at Charlemagne's command.
The rest of her years were lived out in poverty and
misery. Her last days were spent in Pavia where she
begged her bread daily. Asser, wishing to emphasize
the extremities to which wickedness could bring even
a crowned head, added to Alfred's narrative that he

personally had "heard from many who saw her" that in her days as a beggar she was "accompanied by one servant only."[26]

The fact that Alfred, so many years later, should have told in such detail the story of Eadburh and emphasized that her career had stood as a warning to subsequent generations, is sufficient evidence of the impression made on him by what he surely regarded as his father's error. Alfred's subsequent career indicates no hostility toward the idea of rule by a queen, but he does seem to have shared his subjects' belief that, in Wessex, where succession was by election and not solely by heredity, the right to rule should not rest upon so unstable a foundation as a monarch's sexual whim or romantic fancies.

Whether or not he knew what Alfred thought, Ethelwulf was not left in doubt about the views of his eldest surviving son. Ethelbald, when he learned that his father was returning from the continent with a child bride as his co-equal in rule, assembled a force of warriors to prevent the king from re-entering the kingdom. In this move he was supported by all his counselors. They had grievances in addition to the circumstances of Ethelwulf's marriage. He had absented himself from the country for more than a year. He had also "released the tenth part of all his kingdom from royal service and tribute" that all muniments from it might go to the church. A great deal of West Saxon wealth was going to Rome. Some blamed the bishop of Sherborne and the earls of Somerset for influencing the prince to revolt against his father.[27] But Ethelbald was credited by others with being headstrong enough to take the initiative. He, perhaps, had not been as close to his father as Athelstan, now dead, who had campaigned shoulder to shoulder with the king, or Alfred who was reputed to be the favorite son. He doubtless had borne heavy burdens in his father's absence and found insupportable the idea that a mere slip of a girl, a stranger to Wessex, should become his sovereign.

But Ethelwulf had a loyal following among the people. They rushed out to welcome him with joy. Be-

75-7778

sides, the king's actions could be interpreted as clever policy. Beset by invading Danes and other enemies, he had by marriage cemented an alliance with the king of the Franks and had joined to the prestige of his own royal house that of Charlemagne's. Most of the nobles were not prepared to repudiate their king. Civil war seemed inevitable. Ethelwulf had the stronger hand but made the greater concession to preserve the peace. "With the consent of all the nobles, the kingdom was divided between father and son." Old Wessex, the chief seat of power, would be under Ethelbald's rule. The eastern dominions, Sussex, Surrey, Kent, and Essex, would be ruled by Ethelwulf and Judith.[28]

Alfred must have been thankful that war between his father and his brother had been prevented. Asser, who derived much of his knowledge of the controversy from Alfred, described Ethelbald as "unjust, and obstinate" and branded his efforts to prevent his father's return "an infamous deed unheard of in all previous ages." The peaceful settlement he attributed to Ethelwulf's "ineffable clemency."[29]

Ethelwulf died two years later, secure in the affection of his subjects. He seems to have cared little for the possession of great power, but the conditions that caused him to relinquish dominion over the richer half of his kingdom were painfully imprinted on his memory. He left a letter requesting the division of the realm between his two eldest sons and setting forth the exact division of private property among his children "that his sons might not quarrel unreasonably after his death." Characteristically he also generously remembered the poor, providing that one poor man be fed and clothed for every ten hides of cultivated crown lands.

Alfred had lost a companion as well as a father. Ethelbald found a kingdom and wife. Despite Ethelwulf's expressed wishes, Ethelbert, the second eldest son, consented to Ethelbald's rule over both kingdoms. And Ethelbald, at last king of all the lands once ruled by his father, now took to wife a fascinating young woman, the very girl whose marriage to his fa-

31

ther two years before had stirred the wilful son to rebellion. This marriage, contrary both to Christian
custom and the pagan practices which the Saxons had
once followed, outraged Wessex. That there was no
organized rebellion against Ethelbald was a tribute
both to his personal strength and that of the House of
Wessex. Even so, there might have been serious trouble for Ethelbald if Ethelbert had not been peace loving, like Ethelwulf.

It may be surmised that Alfred, now nearly eleven
years old, was more at home in the court after Ethelbert ascended to the throne than he had been in
Ethelbald's reign. One person definitely not at home
was Judith, who returned to France to live in a castle,
a few miles from the scene of her marriage to Ethelwulf. From there, with the aid of her brother, she
eloped to Rome with a lover, Baldwin the Iron Arm.

Ethelbert soon had even more serious problems
than dealing with Judith. In the first year of his reign
the Vikings sailed up river to Winchester and nearly
destroyed the capital. But when they were returning
to their ships under the weight of their booty, two
Saxon earls, leading the men of Hampshire and Berkshire, fell upon them, slaughtered large numbers in a
fierce battle, and put the rest to flight.

Five years of freedom from major assaults by the
Vikings, combined with internal harmony under Ethelbert's benevolent rule, gave the Saxons a period of
greater security than they had known for some time.
In this half decade Alfred grew to manhood. In ninth
century Wessex, a boy who was not a man by his sixteenth year was the object of parental concern.

The adolescent boy became an expert hunter in a
day when such ability was highly regarded both as a
manly art and a means of putting meat on the table.
He could stalk the stag almost silently through the
green depths of the forest and bring him down with
the whirring flight of an arrow. On some of these expeditions he was accompanied by lithe, slender
wolfhounds, deep chested but snake hipped, or by
hawks that circled above their prey with a metrical

grace. Alfred's later writings bear ample evidence that he was alive to the beauties of nature and sensitive to its mysteries as well as exulting in the sheer joy of athletic achievement. It is good that he had this activity. Some accounts indicate that he had more than a normal share of sickness as a boy.[30]

Evenings were spent listening to scops chanting Anglo-Saxon poetry as they plucked their harps. Half historical, half legendary figures battled each other amid swirling mists or stalked monstrous fiends across dark ridges under shifting clouds heavy with menace. Alfred's imagination was excited; his emotions were aroused. If the phraseology of some of Alfred's writings is a clue, he must have been particularly impressed with *Beowulf*, the great epic of his people. Alfred seems to have accepted the ideal of a hero as set forth in that famous poem. He could hardly have found a better model for his time. Beowulf was not only the courageous man of action defending the people from powerful foes; he was also one of the great gentlemen of world literature. When his bitter rival became his friend and lent his sword to Beowulf to do battle with a monster, the great warrior's exquisite courtesy forbade his ever hinting afterward that he had not been able to use the weapon at all. The words of Beowulf's epitaph were to be echoed in Alfred's writing near the close of his life:

> ...kindest of earthly kings,
> Mildest, most gentle, most eager for fame.[31]

Did Alfred, as he approached manhood, dream of leadership in the kingdom? It would not be strange if he did. His imagination fed on heroic literature. He was the brother, son and grandson of kings. Scops at court sang tales of his ancestors going back fourteen generations to Cerdic the Saxon, who had waded ashore in Britain at the end of the fifth century and remained to found the Kingdom of Wessex six years later. Overzealous genealogists, more courtiers than scholars, had traced his ancestry beyond Cerdic to Sceaf "the son of Noah...born in Noah's ark."[32] Appropriate ancestry, indeed, for a man later to be

33

called "the founder of the British navy"! Alfred the
mature historian probably gave about as much cre-
dence as modern scholars do to the accounts of his
genealogy before Cerdic, but Alfred the boy may have
accepted uncritically the tales of ancestral glory
stretching back to biblical times.

In Alfred's sixteenth year Ethelbert died. Even at
the time of personal grief as he stood at his brother's
grave, the third newly dug grave of a West Saxon
king in seven years, he must have reflected solemnly
upon the fact that he, the youngest of Ethelwulf's five
sons, was now the only one remaining except Ethelred, the new king.

When Ethelbald had died, Ethelred and Alfred,
"with the witness of all the councillors of the West
Saxons," had entrusted to their brother Ethelbert, the
new king, all their inheritance "on condition that he
should return it to us as fully at our disposal as it was
when we entrusted it to him."[33] Ethelbert had scrupu-
lously kept his word, returning not only the property
but all profits that he had obtained from the use of it.
Now, in 865, Alfred asked Ethelred before the council
to divide their joint inheritance so that he might have
his share.

"I cannot divide it readily," said the new king, "for
I have very often attempted it. But I will leave after
my death to no person sooner than you whatever I
hold of our joint property and whatever I acquire."

Alfred assented immediately and harmony prevailed. As he said later, "We were all harassed by the
heathen army."[34]

The Vikings had already collected tribute from the
people of Kent upon promise of peace and then, under cover of darkness, ravaged the eastern part of
that sub-kingdom. Now the Great Army of the Danes
landed in England and went into winter quarters in
East Anglia. The East Anglians, aware of what had
happened in Kent but desperate, made peace with the
invaders. The Vikings obviously intended to stay.
Ethelred would need resourceful and dependable
help to combat so formidable a foe. He turned to his

younger brother. And so Alfred, in his sixteenth year, turned from dreams of glory to the assumption of an heroic task. With the consent of the council, he was officially designated *Secundarius*, second-in-command, in the threatened kingdom.[35] In this hour there descended upon his youthful shoulders a large part of the burden of protecting from the barbarian conquest not only Wessex but all of Western Europe.

IV

AFFLICTION
AND REVELATION

*t*he people of Wessex in 866 must have longed
for another Egbert, or even another Ethelwulf
as he was in his prime a quarter century before
when he made "the greatest slaughter among the
heathen host yet heard tell of." Instead, with the
Danes sending their greatest force to England with
the obvious intent of subjugating the island, Wessex
had as leaders an untried king and his sixteen-year-
old brother.

Alfred may well have felt that, like Beowulf, he
faced the necessity of fighting a monster. For the invaders were led by Halfdene and Ivar the Boneless,
sons of Ragnor Lothbrok, the great Viking raider who
sailed up the Seine to Paris, sacking the palace of
Charles the Bald, cutting beams from the church to
repair his ships, and making Easter of 845 memorable
by the murder of 111 prisoners in full sight of the
horrified populace.[1] Halfdene was fierce in the pre-
vailing Norse tradition of athletic rapine. But Ivar the
Boneless was horrible in a special way. Tradition said
that Ragnor's young bride had begged him not to bed
her on their wedding night, saying that if he did not

37

wait three days a curse would befall the child of their union. Impatient of such pleading, he promptly plowed the sobbing girl. Nine months later she gave birth to a child with too much gristle and too little bone in his skeleton. Whatever the degree of truth behind the tradition, the full grown Ivar was weirdly flexible, like an India rubber man. Yet this physical monster harbored a fiendishly clever brain. Ivar, it was said, was the mastermind of the Danish conquest.[2]

Ethelred and Alfred could only conjecture regarding the Viking strategy. Four small kingdoms stood between the Norsemen and subjugation of the island—a prize in its own right as well as an ideal fortress from which to ravage France. One of these kingdoms, East Anglia, they had already occupied. Here they spent a year readying themselves for the great campaign. In the fall of 867 they broke camp. The apprehension which this move stirred in Wessex, in Northumbria, and in Mercia is easily imagined. In selecting East Anglia as a base of operations, the Vikings had chosen well. Its seacoast gave ready access to their fleets of dragon ships; forests and swamps guarded its borders except for the openings to the north from which they could sally forth into Northumbria, those to the west through which they could attack Mercia, and those to the southwest through which they could move against Wessex. On horses furnished them by the East Anglians the Danes rode northward up the old Roman road and ferried across the estuary of the Humber. Northumbria was to be the victim.[3] According to a tradition persistent in Scandinavia, Northumbria was selected because its king had captured Ragnor on his last raid and had thrown him into a snakepit. As the old pirate had writhed, Laocoön-like, in the coils of the serpents, he is supposed to have gasped out before dying: "How the young boars would snarl if they knew how the old one suffers!"[4]

Now, according to the old Scandinavian story, the young boars were snarling for revenge. If the account of Ragnor's torture is true, the desire for vengeance may have heightened the sons' delight in ravaging Northumbria. But there were ample practical reasons for invading Northumbria next in the timetable of conquest. Two centuries before, it had been the most powerful kingdom in Britain. But the internecine quarrels of its royal family had repeatedly resulted in the armed strife which Ethelwulf had been at such pains to avoid and which had been prevented on several occasions by the forbearance of members of the reigning house of Wessex. Only five of Northumbria's fourteen kings in the eighth century died natural deaths while in power. Four were forced from the throne; five were murdered.[5] When the Vikings headed northward up the old Roman road into Northumbria, the kingdom was especially vulnerable. One king had just been driven out, and his successor faced considerable discontent, inspired in part, it is said, by a nobleman who did not feel complimented on learning that in his absence on military duty his wife had been raped by his sovereign. Northumbria collapsed almost as easily as the old Roman walls, long in disrepair, that crumbled on November 1 before the Danish onslaught.[6]

After a year of pillaging and destruction throughout Northumbria in which they beat down an uprising and put their own kept Saxon on the throne, the Great Army in the fall of 867 rode south into Mercia. They encamped at Nottingham, a strategic location both from the standpoint of maintaining control of Northumbria and of moving against the Mercian city of London.[7] The Danish plan of picking off the Saxon kingdoms one at a time was proceeding with uninterrupted success.

Burhred, king of Mercia, who had married Ethelswith, sister to Ethelred and Alfred, soon called on his brothers-in-law for help. In earlier days, when West Saxon kings had acknowledged Mercian overlordship, the call would have been a summons to vassals. It was now an appeal to an equal sovereign and his secundarius to be brothers-in arms. Assembling a large army from all parts of Wessex, Ethelred and Alfred

marched on Nottingham and besieged the Danish fortress there. But the West Saxons were unable to breach
the walls and the Norse wisely refused to come out
and fight. In the resulting stalemate, peace was concluded between the Mercians and the Danes and the
brothers from Wessex rode home with their army.[8]

An abortive venture, surely! But perhaps not entirely so. For it was now, in 868, that Alfred, in his twentieth year, contracted a marriage with a young
woman of Mercia. Ealswith was the daughter of an
earl who, like Alfred's brother, was named Ethelred.
Since her mother Eadburh was a relative of King
Burhred, it is quite possible that Alfred first met the
girl when he answered the Mercian king's plea for
help. If so the courtship must have been swift. And
there is good reason to believe that it was based on
personal attraction. As secundarius, Alfred was beyond having his sovereign arrange for him a marriage
of state.

The wedding took place in Mercia, according to a
contemporary account[9] "in the presence of a great
multitude of both sexes." There was feasting into the
night. The clean-shaven[10] young bridegroom had a
dignity and force of personality that commanded respect. There is every reason to believe that Ealswith
seemed a worthy bride for such a man. Suddenly, in
the midst of all the rejoicing over so promising a
union, Alfred grimaced. Then his features contorted
in agony. He had been seized by almost unbearable
pain. Physicians, summoned then and in ensuing days,
admitted their bafflement.[11]

Physicians and historians today know little more
about Alfred's seizure than the medicine men of his
own day. The clues that have come down to us are
more tantalizing than helpful. We do know that the
affliction would recur so many times that Asser would
write twenty years later of Alfred: "He has not a single hour's security in which he is not either suffering
that infirmity or being driven almost to despair by the
fear of its coming."[12]

Several causes have been suggested, prominent
among them kidney stone, gall stone, diverticulosis, or

some other condition severely irritating the colon. The fact that this attack came upon him on his wedding night, following a day of more than usual excitement and feasting on a great variety of dishes, argues for the last possibility. Strengthening this likelihood is the fact that, years after the first attack, a physician in Jerusalem prescribed a bland diet for him. Partly responsible for the dearth of specific information about Alfred's illness is the disposition of this man, so understanding of disability in others, to regard any physical weakness in himself as something that might render him "contemptible."[13] The great tragedy is that Alfred should have been tortured for so many years by something that modern medicine probably could have cured or, at least, rendered less painful.

Alfred's illness did not incapacitate him except during intervals of the most intense pain. He continued to function as secundarius, second only to the king in council as well as on the battlefield. Ethelred was thankful for the advice and support of his younger brother as he awaited the next move of the Vikings. When spring came the Great Army of the Danes pulled up stakes again. Were they headed for Wessex? To general surprise, they moved back into East Anglia, ravaging with fire and sword. Perhaps the willingness of the West Saxons to enter Mercia to do battle with the Vikings had dashed Danish hopes that Wessex, if invaded, would sue for peace. Edmund, East Anglia's young king, had quickly made peace with them before. They were confident that they had nothing to fear from him now. Great was their astonishment, therefore, when Edmund led an army against them. Unfortunately, he was defeated and killed by the Vikings. According to some reports, he was tied to a tree to serve as a target for Danish bowmen until they put an end to their sport by cutting off his head. Thus East Anglia, like Northumberland, ceased to exist as an independent kingdom. Besides Wessex, only Mercia retained even the semblance of sovereignty.[14]

In December the restless Great Army was on the move again. Would its destination be Mercia or the

41

richer, though more defiant, Wessex? It proved to be
Wessex as the Danes moved into Alfred's native Berk-
shire and encamped just east of the royal residence at
Reading. This position—between the Thames and
Kennet rivers—was protected by water on three sides.
Under the leadership of Halfdene, whose brother
Ivar the Boneless was now apparently chief of the occupation forces in Ireland,[15] the Vikings hastened to
protect the fourth side with an embankment. Two of
the Danish earls leading a foraging party some four
or five miles from camp accidentally encountered a
West Saxon earl with his followers. The Saxon chief
was the same Berkshire earl who had played a large
part in putting the Danes to flight in Ethelbert's reign
after they had sacked Winchester. Once again he
drove his enemies before him, killing one of the Viking earls.

Four days after this skirmish Ethelred and Alfred
led an army against the enemy camp near Reading.
They suffered heavy losses, among them the valiant
earl of Berkshire, without dislodging the Danes. The
passage of four more days saw the entire Great Army
of the Danes and all the power of the West Saxons
confronting each other in full battle array at Ashdown.[16] On that January morning, the Viking forces
were drawn up in two color-splashed and glittering divisions along the higher ground of the chalk ridge,
the gaudiness of their blazoned round shields and
gleam of their weapons in stark contrast to the dead
brown grass that stretched between them and the two
divisions of the much less colorful Saxon troops.
Alfred sat his horse opposite the Viking division led
by the earls, for he was to lead the division opposing
them. His brother Ethelred, besides being in command of the whole West Saxon operation, was to lead
in person the fight against the other Danish division,
which was led by two kings. When Alfred's eyes wandered from the gleaming spear points and raven banners of his foes they were drawn inevitably to the one
object standing above grass level on the barren plain
between the armies—a lone, stunted thorn tree that

somehow accented the forlornness of the scene. He
was not cheered by the fact that the Saxons would
have to fight uphill. And he was disturbed by the fact
that Ethelred had not yet arrived.

The king was still in his tent, completing his morning devotions. He was told that the enemy had assembled in readiness for battle. He replied impatiently: "I
will not leave here alive until the priest has finished
the mass, nor will I leave Divine service for the service
of men."

By now the Vikings were shouting the taunts and
boasts with which they usually prefaced a great battle.
Moreover, a restless movement among the enemy host
presaged an attack. Alfred was only second in command but he was not sure he should permit the advantage of attack to pass to the Danes while he waited
for his brother. The Danes closed their shield wall
preparatory to advance. Alfred shouted to the Saxons
to do likewise. Ethelred was not in sight. Alfred gave
a shout and moved forward—"like a wild boar," one
chronicler[17] said. The two armies clashed around the
stunted thorn. Ethelred rode up to help his brother.
The fight went on for hours. Finally the Danes gave
way, fleeing back to Reading. The Saxons chased
them till nightfall and in some instances till break of
day. The rising sun disclosed the chalk downs strewn
with the bodies of slain Vikings, and glittered on the
gold braceleted arms of five earls and a king. The naked thorn still stood amid the desolation.

Even so loyal a friend of Alfred as Asser was inclined in later years to attribute the victory more to
Ethelred's pious persistence in devotion than to
Alfred's readiness to attack.[18] No great contrast can be
drawn between these brothers in the matter of religion. Like their father, both were religious. But perhaps Ethelred was more like the Ethelwulf who made
a pilgrimage to Rome to save his people and Alfred
was more like the earlier Ethelwulf who in 850 smote
his enemies hip and thigh. Maybe there was more of
Egbert in Alfred than in any other of the great king's
descendants. In any event, the chief significance of

the Battle of Ashdown—far outweighing any immediate military result—was the revelation that Wessex had, in the gentle and bookish younger brother of its king, a bold young leader who would seize the initiative at a decisive moment.

V

OUTMANEUVERED

In terms of immediate military accomplishment, the success at Ashdown was as barren as the field itself. Though Saxon morale profited from the victory and Alfred gained in prestige (and doubtless in personal maturity) as a result of his part in it, these results were not quickly reflected in any shift in the balance of power between West Saxons and Danes. To one who saw the naked thorn tree standing on its arid height, not so much changed by the storms of recent conflict as by the winds of nature, it might seem that the clash of armies had never taken place.[1] The Danes continued to hold Reading, and from this base within two weeks they were raiding deep into Wessex.[2]

The wily Vikings, far more experienced in warfare than Ethelred and Alfred, were discovered in a strong new defensive position protected by the wetlands of the River Loddon, miles from the Reading base where the Saxons thought they had them confined. The royal brothers attacked the position but were forced to retire. Like other commanders of informally organized armies drawn from a rural society—Washington in the American Revolution, Lee in the American Civil War—they were hard put to keep a full fighting force in the field when there were farms to be looked after, and on those farms families that might be victimized by the enemy. The Danes and the Saxons fought no major battle again until a month later at Meretun, probably the site of the present village of Marten, on Salisbury Plain.[3] For the greater part of the day the Saxons seemed to have the better of the fight and hopes rose for a repetition of Ashdown. But a Danish counterattack late in the afternoon gained the field. Among the numerous Saxon casualties was a fighting bishop of Sherburne, one of the Wessex stalwarts. From the position that they held, the Danes could strike at Salisbury, or again at the royal manor of Chippenham, or even Winchester—seat of the royal treasury and the closest thing to a national capital in Wessex, with its peripatetic court.[4]

From London in this dark hour came news that a second Great Army of the Danes had not only landed in England but, while the power of Wessex was occupied in the area of Meretun, had proceeded with impunity to the safety of fortifications at Reading.

In that cruel April of 871 there was yet another event distressing to the Saxons, and especially to Alfred. Ethelred died.

The dead king's sons were too young to be considered as successors. Only one male member of the House of Wessex was mature enough to provide leadership. That man was, of course, Alfred. Under the laws and customs of the West Saxons, succession to the throne was not automatic according to a prescribed order of kinship. The Witan, or King's Council, consisting of the earls and bishops, in effect elected a monarch when it "recognized" a proper successor. Several qualifications were considered, prominent among them the ability of the nominee to provide effective leadership in council and on the battlefield. And, though kingship was not determined solely by kinship, the possession of royal blood was a virtual necessity and close relationship to a predeces-

sor was one way of bolstering the royal office by providing continuity.[5] Alfred was not only the brother of
the deceased king but also his effective secundarius,
or second-in-command. Indeed, at Ashdown, the
great victory now wistfully remembered, Alfred had
played a more decisive role than the king himself. It is
not surprising that, with Ethelred dead and two Great
Armies of the Danes (the greatest combined force of
Vikings ever to invade the island kingdoms) preparing
to crush Wessex, its council should unhesitatingly offer the crown to Alfred.

Alfred was far from exultant. Depressed by the
death of his brother, whose comrade in arms and
partner in council he had been, he was called upon to
defend the kingdom at a time when most of the great
warrior earls had passed from the scene and the enemy threatened in such numbers as his brothers, his father, and his grandfather had never faced. With a
reluctance we may be sure was unfeigned, he accepted
the responsibility thrust upon him. He doubtless took
an oath before the Witan, but there was no time for a
ceremonial coronation.

But, however great his reluctance to assume the
crown, Alfred would be king in fact as well as name.
There was ample demonstration of this when, at the
start of his reign, high placed persons complained of
his disposition of the lands inherited from his father
and brother. The imputation of injustice must have
been particularly galling to Alfred who, five years before, had deferred his own inheritance in the interest
of family and national unity. The matter of the legacy
was a complicated one rooted in the will of King Ethelwulf. Alfred now had this will brought before the
Witan and read aloud.[6] Either because of the new
king's importunity or their concern, "all the councillors of the West Saxons" were present. After the reading, Alfred addressed them:

"I beg you all for love of me— I give my word
that I shall never bear any of you a grudge for declar-
ing what you see to be right—that none of you will

hesitate for love or fear of me to pronounce the common law, lest any man should say that I wronged my young kinfolk."

"I cannot imagine a juster title," said one councillor. There was a general murmur of assent.

One member spoke for all when he said:

"Now that everything in ... [the will] has come into your possession, bequeath it and give it into the hand of kinsman or stranger, whichever you prefer."

To a man they gave Alfred their pledges and their signatures—most of them probably actually only touching in assent the Maltese crosses by signatures written for them by a scribe—that as long as they lived no one should ever change the provisions in any way other than as Alfred himself should decide in his last days.

Alfred's first political crisis had dissolved before his candor and force and determined good humor. He was not one to let troubles fester in the dark.

With unity established within his kingdom, he addressed himself to the problem of defending it against the Danes. Exactly what considerations impelled Alfred to take the steps that he took we can only conjecture on the basis of subsequent actions and of the capacity that he later demonstrated to see events in a large context. He must have perceived that the Danes, tired of mere raiding, were embarked upon a policy of empire building. England lay between the Viking lands of the North Sea and those of Ireland. If the island's two remaining Saxon kingdoms—Mercia and Wessex—were conquered, the northern arc of empire would be complete. The most obvious advantage enjoyed by the Danes was symbolized by their dragon-prowed ships: they indisputably had command of the seas. They had also a huge army, or collection of armies, that lived by fighting and gloried in it, as compared with the Anglo-Saxon *fyrd*, or "national militia," that responded to the king's occasional call more out of duty, discipline, or desperation than eagerness for combat.[7] Whether in ships or on horseback, the Vikings had an astonishing mobility developed by con-

stant practice. They also enjoyed superiority of
weapons.[8] There is reason to think that their swords
were better suited for heavy duty than the more highly ornamented ones of the Anglo-Saxons. Their
spears were at least as good as the iron-headed shafts
of ash carried by the ordinary soldiers of Wessex.
Their heavy throwing axes were feared throughout
Europe. What weapons they could not forge for
themselves, the Vikings had bought or stolen all over
the continent from the North Sea to the Mediterranean.

Faced with so formidable a foe Alfred must have
concluded that the West Saxons' only hope lay in de-
ferring large scale warfare with the invaders until
more effective preparations could be made. Yet the
Danes, who had been quick to take advantage of East
Anglian and Mercian reluctance to fight, must not be
allowed to believe that England's new king would not
fearlessly oppose their designs. At least one major battle would be necessary.

About a month after assuming the throne, Alfred
fought the Vikings at Wilton, on a hill about four
miles west of the present city of Salisbury. Exhausted
by the many fights that caused 871 to be known afterwards as the Year of Battles, and tortured by anxiety
for their families and farms, Alfred's army had melt-
ed away except for "a small band."[9] Despite the limited size of his force, the king more than held his own
in the first hours of battle. But the Danes feigned
flight and the Saxons, as several times before, fell for
the ruse. When the embattled Saxon farmers broke
ranks in the eagerness of their pursuit, the disciplined
Viking veterans turned upon them and won the day.

Alfred had proved that he would fight and had
gained Danish respect, but he realized that to continue fighting against such overwhelming odds as he
faced would be to insure disaster. He negotiated. Asser, fiercely loyal, tells us: "The Saxons made peace
with the pagans on the condition that they should depart from them. And this they did."[10] But our knowledge of the Danes' methods of operation makes it

incredible that they should have left Wessex after gaining the field, unless they were paid to leave. We may be sure that Alfred quite literally bought time.

But he did not buy security, and he knew it. When the Danes left Wessex several months after the battle of Wilton they simply moved down the Thames to London, within easy striking distance. And they clearly did not intend to abandon London. Halfdene began minting coins there with his image on them.[11]

Alfred had at least one advantage over Halfdene. The Danish leader was but the most prominent of a group of chieftains whose coordinated efforts were required to mass the Great Armies of the Vikings. Alfred, on the other hand, held undivided sovereignty over his people and he had been proclaimed king of Wessex "with the approbation of all the inhabitants." The relationship between a West Saxon king and the Witan was loosely defined by custom and varied according to the personalities involved. The genius for compromise which was often to be the salvation of English government had already evolved in Wessex. Under a strong king more compromises were made by the earls than by the sovereign.[12] Alfred, from the first, showed himself a strong king.

Both king and Witan, however, were limited by laws which defined relationships in an aristocratic society in which each man was assigned a precise worth. His value was indicated by the *wergild*, the sum which anyone's slayer was required to pay the victim's family in order to avoid a blood feud. In Wessex a *gesithcund* man, or king's companion, had a wergild of 1,200 shillings whereas the ceorl, or independent head of a peasant household, had a wergild of 200 shillings. The enshrinement in law of these distinctions went back at least as far as the reign of Alfred's collateral ancestor, Ine, who became king of Wessex in 668.[13] But the concept of a nobility consisting of companions to the king was far older than the code of Ine. Tacitus, in the first century A.D., wrote of the special status in Germanic society of the companions to the chieftain, a bodyguard that had become largely hereditary. Readers of *Beowulf* are familiar with the ancient concept of a sacred bond between the chief and his comitates. He deserved their unremitting efforts in his defense; they deserved his generosity. By Alfred's time this relationship was formalized into feudalism with the earl taking an oath of allegiance to his king and the retainers of an earl taking the same oath of allegiance to their overlord:

"By the Lord, before whom these relics are holy, I will be loyal and true to _____, and love all that he loves, and hate all that he hates, in accordance with God's rights and secular obligations; and never, willingly and intentionally, in word or deed, do anything that is hateful to him; on condition that he keep me as I shall deserve, and carry out all that was our agreement, when I subjected myself to him and chose his favor."[14]

The king, of course, was at the apex of the social structure, but that structure was not pyramided from bottom to top with each stratum resting upon a pledge of loyalty from the one below. The ceorl, like the great noble, owed allegiance to no man below the king. He owed his sovereign personal service in the fyrd and the protection of the king's peace extended over his home while he was absent in the performance of military duty: unlawful entry at such a time through the hedges surrounding his dwelling was an especially heinous offense, as was the breaching of a nobleman's walls in similar circumstances. The typical ceorl was a free man whose "free ancestors ... had crossed the North Sea" to England centuries before in the days of tribal organization. Though with no pretensions to nobility, he was every bit as free as the nobles of British descent, who comprised an intermediate class with a wergild of 600 shillings, three times that of the ceorl.[15] In Wessex, as in all of England except Kent, the unit of land division was the *hide*, the acreage deemed necessary to support a ceorl and his household. The unit was variable according to the capacity of the land to support its population, and hence might range from forty acres in Wiltshire to

120 in Cambridgeshire. In most of England the hide
was not only a unit of land measure, but also, logically
enough, the basis for determining the food-rent, the
amount of food which landholders were required to
furnish the king and his retinue as they traveled
about the country and stayed at one royal residence
or another. Responsibility for service in the fyrd, or
national militia, was also proportioned by hides.[16] As
the hide was the unit for so many economic and military determinations in Anglo-Saxon life, so was the
master of the hide, the ceorl, the most stable unit of
society. No other rank was so secure in his position.
Generations of ceorls had tilled their fields as dynas-
ties rose and fell. The ceorl was, like his descendant,
the seventeenth century yeoman in Sir Thomas Over-
bury's description, "lord paramount within himself."[17]

Laws of the Anglo-Saxon period recognized the
right of the ceorl to have slaves. What was then regarded as a guarantee of rights would today, of
course, be considered a denial of them. Many are
shocked to find slavery existing in ninth century Wessex amid some of the inchoate forms of democracy. It
is hard for modern man, aware of all the evils of slavery, to realize that the institution has been, as John
Kells Ingram has said, "a universal and inevitable accompaniment"[18] in the social evolution of nations. The
histories of the ancient Hebrews, the Greeks, the Romans, the Arabians, the Abyssinians all illustrate this
thesis. Both social and economic historians adjudge
that a people have advanced when they stop slaying
their captives and enslave them instead. It is not surprising that West Saxons of the ninth century should
have naively accepted without question a system that
Aristotle had held to be necessary, natural and benefi-
cent and which even the sophisticated Plato had
viewed as natural though awkward. Christianity had
made many West Saxons more conscious of the need
for kindness toward slaves than their ancestors had
been, but the days of concerted Christian agitation
against the institution were still centuries away. If the
individual slave was discontented with his lot his chief

hope lay in manumission as compensation for ill treatment by his master or as a reward for service. Warfare with the Northmen had made many men in bondage more valuable as soldiers than as slaves. Never numerous in Anglo-Saxon society, the slave class had declined proportionately for several generations.[19]

The social picture was complicated by ecclesiastical rank. A bishop was comparable to an earl; lesser clergymen had their lay counterparts. Members of the guard of a king or great earl might technically outrank the ceorl, yet enjoy less independence.[20]

Alfred had his own way of viewing the people of his kingdom, one that cut across barriers of rank to classify men according to their functions. He would one day write:

> ...covetousness and the greatness of this earthly power never will please me, nor did I altogether very much yearn after this earthly authority. But nevertheless I was desirous of materials for the work which I was commanded to perform; that was that I might honorably and fitly guide, and exercise the power which was committed to me. Besides, you know that no man can show any skill, or exercise or control any power without tools and materials—that is, of every craft the materials without which man cannot exercise the craft. These then are a king's materials and his tools to reign with: that he have his land well peopled—he must have praying men, fighting men, and working men. You know that without these tools no king can show mastery of his craft.[21]

Alfred felt the need of the praying men, or clergy, not only to provide moral guidance for his people, but also to keep alive the little formal learning that had survived the Viking assaults on Wessex. Years later, when he had more time for writing, he would write his bishops:

> It has very often come into my mind, what wise men there formerly were throughout England, both of sacred and secular orders; and what happy times there were then throughout England; ... and also the sacred orders, how zealous they were both in teaching and learning, and in all the services they owed to God; and

how foreigners came to this land in search of wisdom
and instruction, and how we should now have to get
them from abroad if we were to have them. So general
was its decay in England that there were very few on
this side of the Humber who could understand their
rituals in English, or translate a letter from Latin into
English; and I believe that there were not many beyond the Humber. There were so few of them that I
cannot remember a single one south of the Thames
when I came to the throne.[22]

Alfred was convinced that he must grow in learning
and wisdom, and so must his people, if they were to
restore England to its former greatness. "For no man
can accomplish any craft without wisdom." The king
determined to exhort his churchmen to greater intellectual labors and to import scholars from the continent to augment the dwindling scholarship of
England's native clergy.

The need for the second of Alfred's classifications,
fighting men, would have been obvious to any sovereign or any subject. The belted earls with their silver-
pommeled swords[23] were needed to captain the armies
that would turn back the Danes, and the ceorls, as
tough as their spears of ash,[24] were needed to fill the
ranks. If the fighting men could not hold their
ground, there would be no need for the scholars.
Reading was not a part of Viking culture.

The workmen, Alfred's third category, were needed
to advance both the arts of war represented by the
kingdom's defenders and the arts of peace represented by the scholars. There was in Alfred an inventiveness that could employ the talents of skilled workmen
in improving the weapons used to fight the invader.
There was also in the king that same aesthetic sense
which had prompted him as a child to memorize his
mother's book of Anglo-Saxon poetry so that he could
claim the manuscript with its glowing initial letter and
shining rubrics. Alfred also remembered with pleasure the columns and noble arches of Rome. And he
delighted in the beauty and intricacy of finely etched
metalwork. When he had the time, he would give per-

sonal attention to the architecture and arts of his
people.

Alfred's concept of his people as tools for his work did not comprehend the whole story of his relationship to them. He saw himself, in an image not yet debased by the unlimited coinage of the hustings, as a servant of the people. The ruler was responsible for providing "land to inhabit, gifts and weapons, and meat, and ale, and clothes, and whatsoever is necessary for the three classes."[25] Alfred was acutely aware that the fulfillment of these responsibilities seemed a doubtful matter. He himself might soon be without a land of his own to inhabit and unsure of obtaining his own meat and ale, to say nothing of providing these things for others. The king might have to become a fugitive.

But Alfred still hoped and worked, keeping a wary eye on the movements of the Danes. Through constant awareness of his people's needs and minute attention to the operations of justice, he promoted the unity of his kingdom. And he did everything he could to gird it for the war that could not forever be deferred. He appears to have concentrated on the building of warships, a very wise course against an enemy that owed so much of its success to sea power, but one apparently neglected by most other rulers, with the exception of Charlemagne, who sought to defend their lands from the Vikings.

The Great Army moved again in the summer of 872, this time into Northumbria, where the people had driven out both their puppet ruler and the archbishop of York. Subduing the populace, the Danes went into winter quarters at Torksey, a town on the River Trent near enough to the Northumbrian-East Anglian border for them to be able to crush an uprising in either kingdom.[26]

Alfred was thankful for each year that Wessex was spared, each year gained for the strengthening of defenses. In the summer of 873 the Danes were content to plunder the lands near their camp at Gorksey. But in the fall they moved into Mercia and set up winter

quarters. Alfred was concerned on several counts: the
movement toward Wessex, the invasion of the only
English kingdom besides his with any pretense to independence, the encampment of the enemy within
the territory of which his sister was queen. Her husband, King Burhred, who had enlisted Alfred's help
twice before in time of Danish invasion, would undoubtedly need it again. The king of Wessex seems to
have considered all the possibilities but one. He did
not foresee that Burhred, who had reigned for more
than two decades under the almost unrelieved threat
of Danish violence, would suddenly conclude that further resistance was useless and flee to Rome. Ethelswith, Alfred's sister, found refuge at his court.[27]

The conquest of Mercia was soon complete. The
Danes placed upon the throne a man named Ceolwulf, an officer of Burhred's household. If the *Anglo-
Saxon Chronicle* may be believed, it was not Ceolwulf's
ability but his pliability that caused him to be so
suddenly elevated. Calling him "foolish," the *Chronicle*
reports that he "swore oaths to [his country's conquer-
ors] and gave hostages that Mercia should be ready
for them on whatever day they would have it and that
he himself and all who would follow him would be
ready for the use of the Danes."[28]

Wessex was now the only English kingdom left to
stand against the Danish might. Help could not be expected from other shores. To the west Dublin had become a great base of Viking power. To the east, the
Vikings had seized the fortified city of Angers in the
Kingdom of the Franks. Charles the Bald had bought
them off but they were prepared to return again and
again in violation of their pledge. The defenders of
Italy were desperately beating back the attacks of the
Saracens. At this moment a great deal of the future of
Western civilization was dependent upon Wessex and
its twenty-five-year-old king.

Now, in the autumn of 874, the Danes made a
move that quickened Alfred's hopes. The Great Army
divided into two, one division returning to Northumbria under Halfdene, the other marching into East
Anglia under the leadership of three chieftains.

Though the three may theoretically have been equals,
one of them, Guthrum, seems at least to have been
"first among equals." Eventually, of course, one of
these divisions would march on Wessex, but facing a
division was preferable to opposing the entire army.
If only the Danes would remain divided! If only they
would hold off for another year!

The Danes under Halfdene were busy building a
strong colony in Yorkshire. A raiding base for pirates
was being transformed into a flourishing agricultural
settlement. The plow had followed the spear. The
other division of the Danish army remained encamped in East Anglia as though poised for an invasion of Wessex. In the summer of 875, while Alfred
was troubled by these land threats, he learned that another Viking fleet was headed for his shores. Here
was a test of his shipbuilding efforts. Alfred put to sea
with his naval force, challenged the seven dragon
ships confronting him, and in the battle that ensued
captured one ship and put the others to flight.[29]

But Alfred was outmaneuvered on land in the autumn of 876. The Danish force encamped in East Anglia slipped past his army and crossed Wessex to the
Dorset Coast, where they took up quarters in the little
town of Wareham, doubtless bringing consternation to
the residents of its nunnery. The location's chief attraction for the Vikings was the fact that it was
bounded by water on three sides. Alfred's small naval
victory had not ended Danish domination of the sea.
Before long, dragon ships from East Anglia floated in
Poole harbor off Wareham. They were joined by other dragon ships from the west, perhaps from South
Wales, perhaps from Ireland. Everywhere on land
fluttered the raven banners of the Vikings. Everywhere along the coasts and up the rivers prowled the
sea dragons. The Golden Dragon of Wessex was almost encircled.

Alfred led his forces to Wareham where the Danes
crouched behind earthworks and stone walls. The
West Saxon siege was inconvenient for the Danes but
they could get supplies by sea. Alfred's hopes of dislodging them were small. Compromise seemed in or-

der. Alfred appears to have paid for peace again. But
this time the king of Wessex demanded and received
as hostages Danish leaders subordinate only to the
three chieftains. Moreover the Viking leaders swore
upon the sacred ring that they would quickly leave the
kingdom. Such a ring, or armlet, ordinarily was kept
in the inner sanctum of a Viking temple except in
time of assembly when it was worn by a chieftain.
Oaths among their own people were sworn upon this
revered object, but the lightly taken vows to men of
other nations had hitherto not been subscribed in this
fashion.[30]

Alfred hoped that this time he had made a lasting
peace with the enemy. The peace concluded after the
battle of Wilton in 871 had not been marked by so
solemn a pledge and it had given Wessex five years
free from invasion. There was reason for hope.

Then one night, when the Saxon Army was lulled
into false security, the Danes swept out of Wareham
and westward toward another coastal town, Exeter. As
soon as Alfred learned what had happened, he sprang
on horseback and galloped after them with a mounted
contingent. But the Danes covered the seventy miles
to Exeter before he could catch them. Fortune, however, was not entirely with the Northmen. While they
waited at Exeter for the dragon ships that had left
Poole harbor off Wantage to join them in an amphibious pincer attack, the crews of those vessels fought a
losing battle against a sudden storm. Many ships were
sunk—120 according to the *Anglo-Saxon Chronicle*.[31]
Perhaps four or five thousand men were lost. The
enemy's most ambitious campaign against Wessex had
failed.

But Alfred still was not able to dislodge the powerful Danish force within the walls of Exeter. He could,
however, keep them confined. By August, they were
ready to make peace, giving Alfred as many hostages
as he demanded, even more than he asked, according
to one account. Alfred breathed more easily as the
Danes withdrew from Wessex, moving into Mercia
and taking up winter quarters at Gloucester.

VI

ISLAND IN THE VOID

If Christmas was not exactly merry for Alfred, it
was at least a time of some relaxation. He was a
lover of the traditions of his people; we may be
sure that the Yule log blazed in the great hall as in
the days of his childhood. The king was later to record his objections to drunkenness, but there must
have been enough quaffing from the silver goblets to
create an inner glow even in guests seated farthest
from the fire and nearest to the wall hangings whose
figures undulated not only in the play of light and
shadow but also in the cold draughts that lifted them.

Above any whistling of the wind in the eaves rose
the chant of the scop, reciting tales of battles with
dragons and miracles of the cross. Like Antaeus,
Alfred derived strength from contact with his native
soil. There was inspiration in the stories, and comfort
in the continuity of mid-winter traditions. There was
also respite from fear of an immediate attack by the
Vikings; even if they should break their word again
they surely would not break the peace so soon after
withdrawing into Mercia and establishing new quarters. Alfred was not overly concerned about having

disbanded the fyrd so that the men could return to
their families. But he never completely relaxed for
long. The painful affliction that had struck him on his
wedding night had returned with such frequency that
he was often in dread of an attack when he was not
actually suffering one.[1] Suppose he should be incapac-
itated sometime when the Danes struck again, as almost certainly they would. As Alfred listened to the
old lays of battles with dragons and of saving miracles,
his mind must have wandered to the dragons that
menaced his kingdom and, as he reflected on their
strength and numbers, he must have wondered if anything less than a miracle could save the nation.

Shortly after Twelfth Night (January 6, 878) the
peace of the holiday season was shattered by the news
that Guthrum, moving as silently as a snowstorm, had
broken camp in Mercia, swept into Wessex, and seized
the royal manor of Chippenham. Before Alfred could
assemble the fyrd, the Danes ravaged the kingdom.
With the king powerless to protect his people from arson, rape, and murder or to provide food and shelter
for them, many of them no longer felt constrained by
any concept of loyalty to him. Hordes of them, some
under the leadership of earls, fled overseas. Many
who remained gave their allegiance to Danish chieftains. Wessex was soon conquered. Alfred had no
fighting force but his personal bodyguard, perhaps
fewer than a hundred men, almost certainly not more
than two or three hundred. He was at last what he
had feared he might become—a fugitive in his own
kingdom.[2] He could be excused for adopting
Burhred's course and fleeing to Rome. Perhaps his
bodyguard expected him to. They may have been sur-
prised when he announced his intentions: he would
hide out, gather followers to him, seek out the weak-
nesses of the enemy, and retake his kingdom.

Alfred's loneliness at this point must have been almost unbearable. Enemies possessed the island that
was his home. Many of his own people were afraid to
help him. Beyond the island shores lay the growing
empire of the Danes and the lands that they plun-

dered. With a laconic eloquence emphasizing both the loneliness of the king's position and the sturdiness of his courage, the *Anglo-Saxon Chronicle* would record:

"The enemy ... occupied the land of the West Saxons and settled there, and drove a great part of the people across the sea, and conquered most of the others; and the people submitted to them, except King Alfred."[3]

Alfred and his supporters did not flee without fighting. According to various Saxon records, more than 800 Danes were killed in Wessex, among them a brother of Ivar the Boneless and Halfdene.[4]

Further open resistance by Alfred became impossible, however. In the words of the *Chronicle*, "He journeyed in difficulties through the woods and fenfastnesses with a small force."[5] Asser is a little more explicit. From him we learn that the king, with a few of his nobles, some soldiers, and a few vassals, dodged in and out among the woods and marshes of Somerset. Alfred learned what it was to go hungry. He and his men survived by taking food in surprise assaults on isolated groups of Danes or seizing provender from West Saxons who had submitted to Danish overlords. Sometimes the meat of the king's campfire was stolen in nocturnal raids on Wessex farmyards in what was now Danish territory. Asser, who had heard Alfred tell of those times, said that the sovereign and his guard "passed a restless time in much anxiety."[6]

At Easter, which in 878 fell on March 23, Alfred dug in at Athelney. It is easy to imagine with what feelings of relief he first saw the island rising like a whale's back above the submerged plain.[7] Most of the year Athelney was merely a forty-foot rise of land, less than thirty acres in extent, surrounded by thickets and swamps. But, with the floods of winter and early spring covering the grassy flats in waist-deep water, Athelney was truly an island. Here Alfred, who was always interested in building, directed his men in the construction of a fort. Housed by their own hands and moated by nature, they were reasonably secure against surprise. Alfred now plotted the recovery of

his kingdom. Small wonder that John Milton once
planned to write a national epic about Alfred's days at
Athelney. How often in history has a philosopher-
king, with his kingdom shrunk to less than the com-
pass of a small farm, successfully planned and executed the rescue of his nation? How often has the
survival of a civilization depended so largely on a fugitive leader in a wilderness hideout in a conquered
country with no prospect of outside aid? An objective
observer might have concluded that the king of Wessex was actuated more by folly than by what Albert
Schweitzer has called "the audacity of genius." Alfred
on the flood-encircled Isle of Athelney seemed to
have as much chance of regaining his kingdom as
Lear on the storm-blasted heath.

Yet from his island fastness Alfred led raids upon
the Danes, swift guerrilla strikes that caught his foes
off balance and reminded his friends that there was
still a king of Wessex, a fighting king.

Alfred could put to good use the hunting skills he
had developed as a boy. Near Athelney other islands
of rush and sedge and thickets of alder rose above the
waters of the Parret marshes. He was surer than most
of his men in bringing down a wild goat or leaping
stag with a swift arrow.[8]

The king foraged for information as well as food.
Legend tells of his entering a Danish camp harp in
hand and disguised as a scop. According to this story
he listened to snatches of boasting between his recita-
tions of heroic lays and learned the battle plans of his
enemies. While this tale is thought to be a twelfth century invention,[9] its details are in keeping with Alfred's
delight in reciting Anglo-Saxon verses to any audience, his passion for seeing things for himself, and his
bold and direct approach to many problems.

Another story told of Alfred's days as a fugitive is
that, dressed as a ceorl, he sought warmth and shelter
beneath a cowherd's roof. The housewife gave him a
seat by the fire, admonishing him not to let her cakes
burn while she was busy elsewhere. The king, absorbed in the problems of rescuing his nation,

thought no more of the cakes until the woman returned to find them burning. "Quick you are to eat
my cakes," she exclaimed, "but you can't move to keep
them from burning! One more time and I'll whack
thee on the nose." Nineteenth century scholars concluded that this story, one of the most popular tales
about Alfred, was a twelfth century creation. Since
then some have traced it to the eleventh century, and
now even to the tenth.[10] The story has been told in
many versions and with increasing elaboration, but
who can say for sure that there is not a grain of truth
at the core of this baroque pearl of fancy? Alfred may
well have dressed humbly to travel incognito among
his people when his safety depended upon concealment. And, undoubtedly, Alfred in humble guise
more than once received less respect than the West
Saxons ordinarily accorded their sovereign. And it
may well be true, as was asserted not many generations after the king's death, that in later life he enjoyed telling of his adventures in the old fugitive days
when he moved in humble disguise among his subjects. Might not memories of these experiences have
influenced him in later years when he wrote that the
rulers of nations should remember that, stripped of
their royal regalia, they were virtually indistinguisha-
ble from other men?

A man of Alfred's philosophical bent must have had
much to reflect upon on clear nights when the mists,
seemingly effulgent in the moon glow, rolled in upon
the moon-flooded Isle of Athelney, breaking against
its sides in slow motion waves infinitely more ethereal
than sea spray, shutting out other rises of land, until
the bright stars above seemed incredibly nearer than
the next human habitation. Enemies lurked beyond
the mist—and friends, too, if they could be found—
but on such nights it must have seemed to Alfred that
he and his little band were alone on an island in the
formless void.

Perhaps it was then that Alfred thought of something that he later wrote: "When a man quits power,
or power quits him, then is he to the universe neither

honorable nor respectable."[11] Or perhaps he thought
then of another comment that he recorded in later
years: "The people's applause is to be held by every
man for nothing, since it comes not to every man according to his deserts, nor indeed remains always to
anyone."[12] In future years, he would, like his sixteenth
century descendant William Shakespeare,[13] celebrate
"the uses of adversity." He asked: "Does it then seem
to you little gain, and little addition to your felicities,
which this severe and this horrible adversity brings to
you: that is, that she very quickly lays open to you the
minds of your true friends, and also of your enemies,
that you may very plainly distinguish them?"[14] Maybe
it was then, too, that Alfred, moved by the loyalty of
simple ceorls as well as belted earls who stood by him
when men of every degree fled the royal presence
and even the native shores, first noted: "True nobility
is in the mind."[15]

Inclined to introspection as he was, Alfred must
have reflected that he had learned at Athelney lessons
that would be invaluable to him as a sovereign—if he
ever regained his kingdom.

But the *if* was fading rapidly from Alfred's consideration. He was cheered by reports of the loyalty of
the fighting men of Devon. A Somerset earl and his
thanes were recruiting more men for the king.
Alfred's own daring raids had lifted the hearts of his
people. The word was being sent throughout the
country-side, passed from earl to coerl to priest, that
the king would meet at Egbert's Stone in the seventh
week after Easter all those who would fight at his side
to drive out the Danes.[16] We do not know what Egbert's Stone was, but it evidently was a marker associated with the exploits of Alfred's grandfather, who in
his time had led the people of Wessex to throw off a
foreign yoke. The spot was well chosen to revive
memories that would unite and inspire the West Saxons.

Almost every day brought reports of new accessions
to Alfred's forces. Though the king still might feel
very much alone on nights when the mists encircled

Athelney, the dawn of each new day, burning away those mists, revealed a world inhabited by hidden friends as well as concealed enemies. The greening of the alders and other vegetation rising from the marshlands heralded the coming of the spring day appointed for the meeting with his people. Keeping pace with the daily changes in the landscape was the greening of the king's hopes.

VII

BATTLE WORM
TO NOBLE STONE

housands of men were gathered on a day in May
of 878 around Egbert's Stone on high ground
near the edge of Selwood forest. At this point the
ancient boundaries of Wiltshire, Somerset, and Hampshire met, and upon this spot had converged many
men from Hampshire and virtually all the able-bodied
men of Somerset and Wiltshire. Some were ceorls.
Some were earls in elegant cloaks held at their shoulders by jeweled clasps that caught the sun. But,
whether they lay upon the ground, sat down, or
paced impatiently, these men of every degree were
united by a common expectancy. No conversation so
engrossed their attention that they did not look up at
frequent intervals.

Suddenly there was a general stir, an outcry, a facing in one direction, a squinting of hand-shielded eyes
turned toward an approaching blob on the horizon
rapidly assuming the lineaments of a party of horsemen. And then to the keenest-eyed the figure in the
forefront was unmistakable. It was their king. They
had been told that Alfred was still alive and they more
than half believed it, but still the fact did not assume

67

full reality until they saw him for themselves. There
was a moment of awe that he should be alive after so
many trials. The time was Ascension-Tide, a season of
great significance for these ninth century Christians,
and many (including those who would have held it
blasphemous to speak of such a thing) must in their
minds have linked Alfred with another who had risen
from the dead. Asser's words have a Biblical echo:

> And when they saw the king they received him like
> one risen from the dead, after so great tribulation, and
> they were filled with great joy.[1]

Silence quickly gave way to cheers. Alfred was dis-
mounted and in their midst. This moment went back
to something earlier in the Saxon experience than
their acquaintance with the Bible. Here was their
chieftain miraculously returned to them like Beowulf
safe from battle in the lair of Grendel's dam. There
had been days when "the gray, old spearmen spoke of
the hero, having no hope he would ever return."
Many of those crowding around Alfred now had, like
Beowulf's followers, "sat grieving and sick in spirit,
stared ... with longing eyes, / Having no hope they
would ever behold their gracious leader and lord
again."[2]

"Many were sure that the savage sea wolf had slain
their leader."[3]

But now he was here "And his mighty thanes came
forward to meet him, / Gave thanks to God they
were granted to see / Their well-loved leader both
sound and safe."[4]

That night Alfred encamped on the spot, sleeping
amid his joyful followers. At dawn he struck camp
and led his army to Iglea, where he again encamped
for a night. The king and his army were on the move
again at the next dawn, seeking a confrontation with
Guthrum's army. It came that morning near Edington, in Wiltshire, on Salisbury Plain. Alfred had suffered one defeat on Salisbury Plain, in the battle of
Wilton shortly after he had first become king. Then
the Danish ruse of feigned flight had demoralized his

army. The king now had disciplined his forces against such a feint. They advanced with shields locked together in a wall and held formation not only in the face of fierce onslaughts but also when the enemy retreated. The Saxons chased the Danes back to the refuge of their fortress. Those unlucky enough to be caught outside were killed by Alfred's army. The Saxons also seized horses and cattle that the Danes did not have time to take within their protecting walls. Thus, when Alfred laid siege to them this time they were not so well prepared for survival as on previous occasions. After two weeks Guthrum sued for peace. He offered Alfred as many distinguished hostages as he wished, said that he expected none in return from the English, promised to leave Wessex, and asked to be baptized a Christian.[5]

Many of Alfred's countrymen must have received this offer with considerable distrust. The Vikings had broken many oaths, even one pledged on their most sacred ring. Though most peoples of Europe, including the Saxon ancestors of the men of Wessex, had long since under Christian influence abandoned violence and rapine as an official way of life, saving them only for special occasions, the Danes continued to rejoice in a religion that exalted the berserker as an ideal of conduct. Surely the only baptism that interested Guthrum was a baptism of blood.

Alfred himself must have had doubts about the Danish king's sincerity. Why should the king of Wessex show mercy on these people who had ravaged his kingdom? Not many days before, Alfred had been a fugitive hunted by them. Now he had a chance to exterminate one of their greatest armies. As word of his triumph at Edington spread throughout the nation his own forces grew daily. He may have been tempted to deal with these people in a way that had never been possible before.

We have no record of the mingled motives which caused Alfred to act as he did. We can only assume that many of his followers must have been dismayed when he accepted Guthrum's offer.

Three weeks later the Danish king and thirty of his
chief men met Alfred at the church at Aller,[6] near the
old hideout at Athelney. There is every reason to believe that the edifice was a stone structure of rude ma-
sonry. But the interior would have presented a
dazzling contrast. Gold and silver altar plate gleaming
in chiaroscuro richness against the shadowy back-
ground of purple wall hangings must have been mo-
mentarily tempting to men who had just abandoned
thievery. The smells of wax and burning incense must
have added to the atmosphere of strangeness for
these freebooters who had generally swept through
churches with a speed that allowed little time for detailed observation. There stood Guthrum and his thirty companions, as immaculate in their white robes as a
choir of angels. Penitent or predator, Guthrum was a
leader. When he decided to be baptized, he decided
all his chief men would be too. Alfred stood as godfather to the old pirate, giving him the Saxon name of
Athelstan, or "noble stone," a fair exchange for Guthrum, which meant "battle worm." Alfred himself
raised the new convert from the baptismal font. Following anointment with the chrism, or oil, of consecration, Athelstan-Guthrum's head was bound with a
white cloth. The robes and the head binding were
supposed to be worn for eight days after the ceremony.[7] Some of the Saxons must have speculated whether the Danish king's reformation would last that long.

The unbinding of the chrism, itself a solemn ceremony, took place in due time at Wedmore, one of
Alfred's royal residences—for Alfred entertained the
Danish king and his followers for twelve days. And, as
the *Anglo-Saxon Chronicle* says, Alfred "honored him
and his companions greatly with gifts."[8]

Even when Athelstan-Guthrum and his followers
rode away after twelve days of royal entertainment,
some of the Saxon king's most loyal subjects must
have feared that Alfred had been naive. Alfred had
worked to build communication between Saxon and
Dane, and, in the words of modern diplomacy, to de-
vise a viable arrangement for coexistence of the two

conflicting cultures. But could a "battle worm" be transformed so quickly into a "noble stone" in the new structure of peace? Alfred himself must have wondered about the success of his experiment in summitry.

His doubts tortured him when he learned that another fleet of dragon ships had sailed up the Thames and that these invaders had debarked and encamped at Fulham. They were reported to be in communication with Guthrum. But these Danes left England for the continent in the next autumn. And Guthrum, far from abetting them, had withdrawn into Western Mercia and at last into more distant East Anglia. His people seemed to be settling down as farmers. Apparently the old pirate was indeed ready to embrace respectability.

Alfred's achievement is perhaps unique in medieval and modern history. Without the aid of foreign allies this man, a fugitive in his own country, lord only of his tiny island lair with its improvised fortifications, had raised an army from a disheartened people and led it to victory against their conquerors, a mighty force strongly entrenched, with powerful allies and control of the seas surrounding the area in dispute. Moreover, with a statesmanship rare in his time, he had envisioned a solution of the problem of Danish threats through a course other than either the annihilation of his enemies or submission to them. He had moved from strength to an accommodation with them. The agreement with Guthrum was, of course, not binding on other Viking armies that might invade England. There was no assurance even that Guthrum himself would be restrained by it for long. But he had abided by its terms for a year in the face of temptations to join forces with a new army of Viking invaders. There would doubtless be reverses, but a start had been made toward a viable alternative to almost continuous war.

The significance of Alfred's achievement is more
readily seen when viewed in the context of ninth century Europe. Danish attacks on the Kingdom of the
Franks multiplied in number and intensity. In 882,
Hincmar, the archbishop who had married Alfred's
father and stepmother, fled before the Viking advance on Reims. Three years later the Danes were at
Paris. In 886, the Emperor Charles, nephew of
Charles the Bald, capitulated to the northern invaders. In 888 he was driven into exile by the nobles of
his own realm, and the corpse of the once great Carolingian Empire was torn apart by petty tyrants. Not
by northern barbarians alone was European culture
threatened. It reeled under assaults by a rival civilization to the south. In 882 Pope John VIII wrote from
Rome:

> ...We dare not leave the walls of our city. Over us
> rages a storm of assault intolerable, beyond endurance.
> Neither our spiritual son, the Emperor, nor any other
> man of any nation appears for our aid. We see advanc
> ing upon us an army, not twofold, but even threefold,
> fourfold. Unless high Heaven comes to our rescue, ...
> we shall be driven captive beneath their yoke. ...

Paris, the capital of the Holy Roman Empire fell beneath the Viking's axe. The capital of the ancient empire of Rome was within the arc of the Saracen's
scimitar. Everywhere Western civilization was at bay—
except in Alfred's Wessex.

VIII
FIRST KING OF ENGLAND

lfred was astute enough to see that the defense of
Western civilization was a threefold task. It involved, first, the peaceful settlement of conflict
where feasible and, second, battle readiness both as a
prop of peace and a preparation if peace should fail.
But it also involved a third concern, overlooked by
most of the king's contemporaries—the active nurture
of all the arts that lift men above barbarism. Too
many defenders of civilization had ironically become
barbarians in its defense.

The pattern of Alfred's attempts to reach peaceful
accomodations with the Danes was established by his
settlement with Guthrum in 878. He had fought skillfully and hard to defeat the Viking king and, having
driven him to surrender, had made him a most generous offer of friendship. The temptation to seek revenge after triumph following so soon upon days as a
hunted fugitive would have been irresistible to a lesser
man. Implicit in Alfred's policy was Churchill's pre-
scription: "In war, resolution; in defeat, defiance; in
victory, magnanimity; in peace, good will."[1] For
Alfred this policy involved acceptance of Danish set-

73

tlement in designated areas of England. There was
the risk that Danish settlers would aid Viking invaders
but there was also the possibility that sea rovers
turned farmers might help to defend the island
against marauders.

Diplomacy to foster and preserve peace was necessary not only in relationships with the Danes, but also
with another Anglo-Saxon kingdom. Mercia, though
shrunken by Danish settlement of its eastern portions,
was still an independent nation of sorts, thanks largely
to Alfred's exertions. It was important to prevent this
surviving kingdom from being absorbed by the Danes.
To a West Saxon ruler of unsophisticated mind, an-
nexation would probably have seemed the simplest solution. The old dynasty had ended and the country's
defenses had been repeatedly breached by the enemy.
Alfred, however, knew that the simplest solution is
not always the easiest. The remembrance of a great
tradition both inhibited the Mercians' acceptance of
change and increased their sensitivity to slight. The
eighty-two years since Offa's death had not erased
recollection that the great Mercian king had dealt as
an equal with the greatest of the Holy Roman Emperors.[2]

Alfred demanded no allegiance from the Mercians.
He simply lent a good deal of help and encouragement to Ethelred, a Mercian earl of proven military
ability who had been closely associated with the old
dynasty. The king of Wessex let it be known that the
people of Mercia would have his protection and that
he found it easy to work with Ethelred. By a process
so gradual that it is impossible to name the starting
date, Ethelred became the administrator of Mercia
with Alfred as his overlord.[3]

But diplomacy, however skillful, could not completely keep war from Wessex. In 882, the Danes penetrated far into the Frankish Empire along the
Meuse, thus incidentally strengthening bases of operation across the channel from England. When Danish
ships appeared menacingly off the coast, Alfred himself put out to sea with ships to forestall a landing.

Fighting against four of the Viking vessels, he killed the crews of two and inflicted so many casualties on the others that they surrendered. The four Viking dragon ships were shepherded into port by the Golden Dragon of Wessex.[4]

Alfred fully realized that a large Danish army was likely to sail for England when the Vikings had thoroughly ravaged the coasts of France and experienced some difficulties in inland penetration. He prepared for that day. Like Charlemagne and the Spanish Moors he saw that the best defense against the Danes was in naval power sufficient to prevent their landing. He therefore began building a navy. Since it was impossible to prevent landings everywhere along England's coasts, preparations had to be made for a more effective defense on land than had hitherto been developed. Remembering how difficult it had been to dislodge the Danes from fortifications, Alfred began the construction of burhs, or fortified communities, throughout his kingdom. Recalling the bitter winter of 877/78 when Guthrum had made him a fugitive because the disbanded fyrd could not be assembled in time, and mindful of other occasions when he was deprived of mobility or concentration because the embattled farmers returned home for harvest, Alfred reorganized the national militia, dividing it in two so that one half of his forces would be in the field at all times.[5]

One might think that Alfred would have used the captured Viking ships as models for his new navy. After all, the Vikings were the greatest boat builders in Europe and their functional accommodation of wind and wave had produced vessels whose sleek lines represented artistry as well as craftsmanship. Alfred, of course, did learn from these great shipwrights. But he would not be a slavish copyist. He would continue to experiment in hopes of improving on the Viking models.[6]

The reorganization of the fyrd was quickly accomplished. The policy of keeping in the field half the men liable for national service while permitting the

others to remain at home had decided advantages.
Since the two divisions alternated no one could justly
complain of inequity. One of the chief problems of
Anglo-Saxon defense had been the vulnerability of
the land when the fyrd was disbanded. Now a standing army was on duty at all times. One of the chief
frustrations of West Saxon leaders had been the restricted mobility of their armies because of the unwill-
ingness of the men to serve outside their own districts,
especially when Danish raiders might strike at their
undefended homes. Under the new system, no district
would be completely denuded of its fighting men.
Though they might claim descent from the gods,
none of the Anglo-Saxon kings had been powerful
enough to command the cooperation from the peasantry that Alfred gained by consideration for their
domestic concerns. As a result, Alfred was able to exe-
cute military operations of a scale and complexity impossible for his predecessors in his own kingdom and
his counterparts in the others.[7] The new system had
the additional advantage of permitting continuity of
operations without neglect of the agricultural activity
necessary to feed the army and the people.

The building of a network of fortifications was a
much slower process than reorganization of the fyrd.
It was made slower than necessary by the peasantry's
lack of enthusiasm for labor on defenses when they
were not under immediate threat of an attack, their
attitude being analogous to that of the householder
who sees no need to repair his leaky roof on a sunny
day. Some of Alfred's greatest frustrations resulted
from his inability to infuse these workers with his own
zeal. Nevertheless he persisted in the building of fortified communities, even planning construction that
would be completed by his successor. The plan was an
ambitious one. Each burh, besides being designed as a
fortress to repel attack, was also supposed to be large
enough to provide refuge for residents of the area in
time of invasion. When the system of burhs was complete, no village in Sussex, Surrey, or all of Wessex
but Cornwall would be more than twenty miles from a

fortress. Alfred was resourceful in employing both natural advantages and surviving works of man, varying the designs of the fortresses rather than constructing them to the Procrustean demands of a masterplan. At some sites, he appears to have utilized Roman ruins whereas in another location a single line of earthwork across a promontory might suffice. Where the landscape offered no special advantages, natural or artificial, the fortress was a rectangle of earthworks surrounded by a ditch. Eventually Alfred worked out a system for manning the fortresses, with four men assigned to a specified length of wall and each hide in the district required to furnish one member of the garrison.[8] Who says that organization was introduced into England by the Normans?

Alfred had only about three years after his small naval victory to advance his plans for general defense before a Danish onslaught in force. The Great Army that had been ravaging the continent flung itself across the channel and besieged Rochester. Alfred's navy obviously was not large enough to safeguard the coast. His system of fortifications was still mostly in his head. But, thanks to his reorganization of the fyrd, the army was ready. When Alfred and his troops suddenly appeared at Rochester, the Danes ran to their ships, leaving behind their horses and their prisoners. Part of the enemy forces sailed back to the continent. The others remained in England on Alfred's terms, which apparently included their staying north of the Thames. But a new crisis presented itself. Perhaps the Danes in East Anglia were so excited by the proximity of an invading army of their countrymen that Guthrum could no longer restrain them. Or perhaps Guthrum himself had grown restless in respectability. For whatever reasons, the Danes in East Anglia broke the peace by giving aid to their countrymen when they violated the Rochester agreement by raiding south of the Thames.[9]

Alfred was not dismayed. He had always realized that this might happen. His course in dealing with Guthrum had certainly been justified by more than six years of peace. The task now was to deal quickly and vigorously with the immediate threat, if possible in a way to derive some permanent advantage for Wessex. The details of the campaign that followed are lost to history. We do know that Alfred seized the initiative, making good use of the increased mobility and improved esprit de corps of the fyrd. He also sent a naval force from Kent to East Anglia. Attacking sixteen Viking ships in the mouth of the Stour, Alfred's force captured all of them and sailed homeward heavily freighted with booty and overconfidence. They sailed into a fleet of Viking ships from East Anglia and were defeated.[10]

On land, however, Alfred was gaining impressive successes. Again the details are unavailable. Asser tells us that Alfred occupied, restored, and repopulated the city of London "after the burning of cities and much loss of life."[11] The *Anglo-Saxon Chronicle* marks the events of 886 in England with a laconic entry:

> King Alfred occupied London; and all the English people that were not under subjection to the Danes submitted to him. And he then entrusted the borough to the control of Earl Ethelred.[12]

Behind the words lies much vital history. Though Winchester was the nearest thing to a capital of Wessex in those days when there were many royal manors and sovereignty resided with a peripatetic king, London already bade fair to surpass it in importance. Its accessibility to the ocean traffic, combined with its position as a hub of roads dating back to the Roman occupation, forecast a return of the days when it had been, in the words of the Venerable Bede in the eighth century, "the market of many nations." Its strategic value was manifest. Its political future was suggested by the fact that, lying within Danish Mercia, it was near the juncture of East Anglia, Kent, and Wessex. Danish possession of London—and the Vikings may have held it continuously since Halfdene's occupation in 872—was both a strategic threat to Wessex and a virtually insuperable impediment to the realization of Alfred's dreams of a united Anglo-Saxon civilization. Evidently London was won at great cost, but London's value was measureless. To Alfred the destruction was only the unhappy prelude to building. And, thanks to his own foresight in preparation, he had in Earl Ethelred an able Mercian prepared to govern the city as his deputy.

The fact that, upon Alfred's occupation of London, "all the English race" free from Danish rule "submitted to him," makes 886 one of the great dates of English history. Other Anglo-Saxon kings had by force of arms obtained the submission of neighboring kingdoms. It was thus that Alfred's grandfather, Egbert, had obtained the title bretwalda, or ruler of Britain. But Alfred did not impose his rule on the other Anglo-Saxon kingdoms. They did not acknowledge him as conqueror; they sought him as protector. Alfred was to be styled *Rex Anglorum*, king of the English. Despite the technicalities which they violate, they do not err in substance who call Alfred the first of England's kings.[13]

Now that he was ruler of all England not held by the Danes, he sought to define the boundary between Anglo-Saxon and Danish territories. For this purpose he met once again with Guthrum. As master of London and undisputed leader of the Anglo-Saxon kingdoms, Alfred was a far more powerful figure than when he had negotiated with Guthrum in 878. On the other hand, King Guthrum, who now ruled East Anglia, was much more a man to be reckoned with than the Danish chieftain defeated at Edington. So Alfred appealed to Guthrum, as an equal sovereign, to meet with him to discuss ways to avert future conflict between their peoples.

The determination of an exact boundary for the Danish kingdom of East Anglia was foremost among Alfred's objectives at this conference.[14] This talk was complicated by the fact that there was no obvious natural boundary. Other questions were related to the boundary. How should charges of border robbery be dealt with? And, since Teutonic justice, whether Danish or Saxon, assigned a precise monetary value to each man, what would be the relative value of each rank of the separate peoples in courts of law?

When Alfred and Guthrum met to discuss these questions, the Anglo-Saxon king had taken steps to insure that any treaty arrived at would be more than a personal agreement between two mortal leaders. He evidently brought with him the witans of Wessex and her sister kingdoms. The agreement[15] was drawn up between "the English nation" and "all the people who dwell in East Anglia." Alfred is described in the document as acting with *Eales Angelcynnes witan*, "the councillors of the English nation." Here, incidentally, was undoubtedly the first formal written recognition of Alfred's new status as king of the English. Both kings confirmed the agreement with "oaths on their own behalf and for their subjects, both living and unborn."

The first clause of the treaty defined the boundary between Alfred's England and the Danelaw, as the country of Danish settlement was called. The line ran "up the Thames, and then up the Lea, and along the Lea to its source, then straight to Bedford, and then up the Ouse to Watling Street." Watling Street, of course, was the old Roman road from London to Chester, a thoroughfare so well built that much of it is in use today.

Alfred's greatest powers of persuasion may have been needed to win his own countrymen's assent to the second clause:

> If a man is slain, whether he is an Englishman or a Dane, all of us shall place the same value on his life— namely eight half-marks of pure gold—except the [English] ceorls who live on tributary land and the Danish freedmen. These also shall be valued at the same amount in either case—that is, at 200 shillings.

On face, this clause represents a generous concession on the part of the English. If we accept the medieval framework in which men were assigned values according to rank, we must concede the fairness of assigning equal value to the lives of Danes and Englishmen of corresponding ranks. But most assuredly the Danish freedman was not comparable in status to the English ceorl, and by no stretch of the imagination did the simple Danish freedman enjoy a position equivalent to that of the English thane. Alfred doubtless thought it wise to sacrifice something on these points to gain agreement. We must remember that Guthrum was conceding a great deal in accepting these terms; Danish tradition held that the slaying of a Dane by a foreigner could be redressed only by the execution of two foreigners. The surprising thing is not that the formula devised was inequitable but that it was worked out at all.

The third clause provided for uniformity of trial procedure in cases of homicide involving both English and Danes, and in every suit between them involving "an amount greater than four mancuses," the mancus being a gold coin worth about 30 pence.

The fourth clause required that a warrantor, or witness, be present at every transaction between Englishman and Dane resulting in purchase of slaves, horses, or oxen. The value of this provision in helping to prevent serious disputes that might imperil the peace is obvious.

The fifth and final cause reads:

> And we all declared, on the day when the oaths were sworn, that neither slaves nor freemen should be allowed to pass over to the Danish host without permission, any more than that any of them [should come over] to us. If, however, it happens that any of them, in order to satisfy their wants, wish to trade with us, or we with them, in cattle and in goods, it shall be allowed on condition that hostages are given as security for peaceful behavior, and as evidence by which it may be known that their backs are clean.

—an Anglo-Saxon way of saying "that no treachery is intended."

When Alfred rode back home from the conference, he had no way of knowing whether Guthrum would keep the treaty. The Danish king had violated an earlier agreement, but, on the other hand, he had kept it for six years despite great temptation. At the meeting just completed, Alfred had treated Guthrum as a legal sovereign and a man of dignity and honor. If the English were fortunate, the old pirate would value the role. At this point we seem justified in looking ahead to what Alfred could not know. Guthrum would never violate the great treaty. When death claimed him in 890 he would have earned the ultimate mark of a secure place in the establishment—a respectful obituary in the *Anglo-Saxon Chronicle*:

> And the northern king, Guthrum, whose baptismal name was Athelstan, died. He was King Alfred's godson, and he lived in East Anglia and was the first [of the Danes] to settle that land.[16]

Alfred did know when he rode back home after concluding the treaty that, whether or not Guthrum kept his word, England would have to repel Danish invaders. There was no way of making peace with all the Vikings in the world. There would be raids and some day there would be another Great Army borne to England by dragon ships. In preparation for that day he would continue to build an English navy and to construct his network of burhs. And he may even have improved the design of English swords. At the start of Alfred's wars, his people's swords were distinctly inferior to those of the Danes, and indeed of Western Europe in general. But during his reign English armorers began to taper the blades as the Danes did and actually to improve on the Viking sword by designing a curved guard and pommel that made the English weapon easier to handle than its Danish counterpart.[17] Perhaps these improvements were initiated by Anglo-Saxon craftsmen in the wave of creativity associated with Alfred's stimulus to national pride. But, since Alfred was interested in metal work and design and was zealous to improve his country's defenses, there is a strong possibility that he had a direct hand in these advances.

By the end of 887, Alfred had astonishing achievements to his credit. Nine years after being a fugitive, the master of less than thirty acres in an England overrun by the Danes, he was recognized as king of the English, having cemented Mercia as well as Kent to his own Wessex. He had joined the Midlands to the southern kingdoms. He had defeated a great Viking army and brought it to terms that included a Danelaw with clearly defined boundaries (roughly England east of a line running from London to Liverpool), agreement on trading regulations to prevent border disputes and judicial proceedings to prevent blood feuds, plus protection for English residents of the Danelaw. He had reorganized the armies of Wessex to gain a mobility and continuity of operation never before attained. He was building a navy that already had won victories against the greatest seafighters of the age. He had either inspired or guided developments that carried his people from a position of inferiority in weaponry to one of equality moving toward superiority. All of these things he had accomplished despite the frequent recurrence of a painful affliction. And now he was wholeheartedly accepted as king of the English in a way that no other man had ever been. If Alfred had never achieved anything else after his thirty-eighth year he would deserve to be honored as the greatest king that had yet lived in England and one of the greatest Englishmen of all time.

Nevertheless he was not satisfied. In defending Western civilization, in his island, he had set himself a threefold task. Two of these labors were well advanced: the peaceful settlement of conflict where feasible, and improvement in battle readiness both as a prop of peace and a preparation if peace should fail. Scarcely begun was the third work necessary for civilization's defense: the active nurture of all the arts that lift man above barbarism. To this enterprise Alfred now addressed himself with the energy, resourcefulness, and creative intelligence that he had hitherto given to war and diplomacy.

IX

"ONE MAN IN HIS TIME..."

*t*o a degree unmatched in medieval and modern history, Alfred energized every major activity of his people. Though his labors as a translator were so vigorous and effective that he became the father of English prose and infused it with so much of his vitality that its literary tradition is the oldest of any modern language in the Western World,[1] his writings were only part of a program for fostering the arts of civilization with which he wrought a cultural revolution in his kingdom.

Revolutionary in social as well as cultural implications was the educational policy which he enunciated in his preface to the *Pastoral Care*: "Let all the free-born youth now in England who have the ability,[2] be set to learning, so long as they are unfit [too young] for other occupations, until in the first place they can read English writing. Let those afterwards be taught the Latin tongue who are to be educated further, and raised to a higher estate."

The free schools founded by Alfred apparently disappeared at the time of the Norman conquest if not before. A government of England was not again to assume responsibility for the education of the masses until the Elementary Education Act of 1870, almost exactly a thousand years after Alfred came to the throne.

The king did not just delegate responsibility for education and then forget about it. He established a court school where the offspring of nobles and freemen were educated with his own children. Characteristically, he closely followed the activities of this classroom under his own roof, supplying many of his own pedagogical ideas, probably more than the teachers wanted.

Asser records Alfred's insistence that Old English poetry be part of the curriculum.[3] Since the king loved to declaim the verses learned in his youth, one is tempted to picture him reciting some of the more sonorous lines during a royal visit to the classroom.

Alfred carefully directed the education of his own children, wisely allowing for individual differences of temperament. Ethelflaed, the eldest, was prepared no less than her brothers for a role of leadership. The king's wisdom in this matter was vindicated when, as Lady of the Mercians, she earned a place in history in her own right as conqueror of the Danes and in the service of ideals and objectives to which her father had devoted his life. Edward, the next born, was destined to be one of England's greatest kings. Aelfryth, particularly encouraged in gentle pursuits, later married the count of Flanders and helped cement an important continental alliance. Ethelgifu, strongly imbued with the religious strain so prominent in the annals of the House of Wessex, would later use her Latin as abbess of a convent founded by her father. Ethelweard, youngest of the children, had a passion for books, which Alfred carefully nurtured, apparently coveting for his son the opportunities for uninterrupted study which the king himself had wanted. The boy became a scholar, rather than a military or political leader, and there is no indication that Alfred wished another destiny for him. All of Alfred's children appear to have been exceptionally intelligent. Their intellectual promise must have been especially gratifying to the father who so loved to learn and to teach.

Alfred was a companion not only to his own children but also to their fellow pupils. Though he might occasionally pop in disconcertingly to demand a recitation and always expected excellence, especially from his own offspring, he also sometimes declared a holiday and led a troop of youngsters on an adventurous expedition into the forests. Altogether, the court school appears to have been a lively place.

The king was not content that the young alone should learn to read. Inquiring into unjust decisions that were appealed to him from courts presided over by earls, he learned that errors frequently were the result of ignorance rather than malevolence or cupidity. Many of the judges could not read. With these officials, Alfred was adamant: "Study the law or quit your office. Such are my commands." Middle-aged and elderly men who had long given more attention to the conformation of a hunting dog than to the conformities of the law, men whose eyes squinted from following the distant gyrations of a hawk rather than the close linear monotony of a manuscript, now became earnest if unwilling students. Some sat as pupils to their own sons. Others, lacking suitable tutors in their families, had to call in ordinary freemen educated in Alfred's schools, employing them, Asser says, "to recite Saxon books before them day and night...lamenting with heavy sighs that they had never attended to such studies in their youth."[4] Probably they also muttered to themselves about the hardheadedness of a king who had brought them to such a humiliating expedient.

Though Alfred had to resort to stern firmness to motivate these laggard scholars, he seems generally to have promoted learning through the contagion of his own enthusiasms. Much was due to his force of personality, but of course thrones, in all matters of fashion, are notable centers of contagion.

The king's enthusiasm for architecture and the graphic arts seems to have been as infectious as his love of learning. Asser tells of the tremendous build-

ing program which Alfred launched[5] and archaeology
confirms his report.[6] Each new fortress tended to become the nucleus of a town, so that the transition
from burh to borough was social as well as ortho-
graphic. Under Alfred's inspiration and occasionally
his direction, churches and villas were constructed.
Alfred himself was sometimes the architect. Though
stone buildings had been constructed in Anglo-Saxon
England at least as early as the sixth century, timber
had continued to be the principal building material,
even for the large structures, well into Alfred's reign.
After 886 the king inaugurated a great program of
building in stone, importing builders and craftsmen
from the continent. As the eminent architectural historian E. A. Fisher has pointed out, "the result was a
new beginning in Saxon church architecture, based on
Carolingian motifs, though by no means a copy of a
foreign style but a truly national English development
which continued to develop until the Norman Conquest."[7] The style was eclectic. Roman influence evident in the rounded columns and double-arched
windows may have come entirely through the Carolin-
gians or partly, as Fisher and others have suggested,
from Alfred's memories of Rome. Sculptural motifs
were sometimes adapted from the Irish and the
Danes. Carved decoration and details of fenestration,
in many instances, appear to have been inspired by il-
lustrations in illuminated manuscripts. It is easy to
imagine Alfred, who had loved them since childhood,
getting many of his ideas from these sources. Square
towers continued to be a characteristic feature of the
Anglo-Saxon church. The double belfry window with
a central column, or mid-wall shaft, helping to support double arches was used with increasing frequency. Both ecclesiastical and royal buildings were now
sometimes two stories high. Triangular-headed door-
ways and windows were an interesting variation from
the arches. Strip work paneling in stone produced interesting patterns on blank walls. Long and short
quoins, the alternation of tall upright stones and
broad flat ones in construction of the corners of
buildings, added further architectural interest.[8]

Alfred's buildings were far from the soaring glory of Gothic, but their earth-hugging architecture had a homely charm of its own.

Alfred's encouragement to the development of a native architecture was continued by his son Edward the Elder and grandson Athelstan. The durability and appeal of the work of Anglo-Saxon builders is today testified to by such survivals as the tower of St. Peter's Church, Barton-on Humber, as well as by the ancient structures all but hidden by additions of much later vintage or transformed by Norman fenestration. As late as 1934 A. W. Clapham wrote, "It is often assumed that Saxon architecture was a poor stunted growth, without the seeds of expansion, and that we owe to the Normans our rescue from an artistic stagnation out of which it was vain to hope for salvation."[9] In the nineteenth century and first decades of the twentieth some Anglo-Saxon buildings were mistakenly credited to the Normans, and earlier, more primitive Anglo-Saxon structures were contrasted unfavorably with the supposed achievements of the invaders. But the researches of Clapham, Fisher, and the indefatigable Taylors (H. M. and Joan) have redressed the balance, revealing the vitality of the architecture and related arts nurtured by Alfred and his Wessex successors. Many scholars now endorse Clapham's estimate: "...in the minor arts the Norman Conquest was little short of a catastrophe, blotting out alike a good tradition and an accomplished execution, and setting in its place a semi-barbaric art which attempted little and did that little ill."[10]

Historians still are puzzled by Asser's reference to gold and silver buildings constructed by Alfred.[11] Some have dismissed the allusion as rhetorical exaggeration even though the Welshman appears to have been painstakingly accurate in recording many details. William Henry Stevenson is perhaps nearer the truth in suggesting that Asser's words "have some narrower sense than the literal one. Possibly he intended to refer to the use of the precious metals in sacred edifices." Ansegis, ninth century abbot of Fontanelle, is supposed to have gilded a spire of the abbey. Golden

doors are supposed to have adorned the basilica of St.
Alban in the palace complex at Ingelheim.[12]

Certain it is that Alfred's people were skilled craftsmen in gold and silver. The ornaments and candelabra which his father carried to Rome excited
connoisseurs in the imperial city. The treasures
unearthed at Sutton Hoo in the twentieth century
have excited connoisseurs of our own time.

Alfred actively fostered artistry in precious metals,
and not alone for the adornment of public buildings.[13]
Concerned as he was with the design of his new fortresses, he had time also to consider the design of a
new brooch. And he gave attention to work in cloi-
sonné and precious stones.

The king has been credited both with much of the
borrowing from other cultures that enriched his country's art and with the restraint that "deterred Englishmen from overgreat enjoyment of the extravagances
of Scandinavian carving, then at work in Ireland."[14]
Whether or not the results of Alfred's influence may
be determined so precisely, it is quite possible that—
given his position, his energy, and his interest in design—his taste affected other arts in his time with
something approaching the transformation that he
wrought in architecture.[15]

Amazed at the time and energy that Alfred found
for a multitude of duties and interests, Asser wrote:

> In the meantime, King Alfred, during the frequent
> wars and other trammels of this present life, the inva-
> sions of the pagans, and his own daily infirmities of
> body, continued to carry on the government, and to
> practice hunting in all its branches; to teach his work-
> ers in gold and artificers of all kinds, his falconers,
> hawkers, and dog-keepers; to build houses majestic
> and good, beyond all the precedents of his ancestors,
> by his new mechanical inventions; to recite the Saxon
> books, and especially to learn by heart the Saxon
> poems, and to make others to learn them. And he
> alone never desisted from studying most diligently, to
> the best of his ability; he attended the mass and other
> daily services of religion...He was affable and pleasant
> to all and curiously eager to investigate things un-
> known.[16]

There were not enough hours in the day for all this activity, so he had to measure the hours of the night as well. Besides, he had vowed to devote half of his time to God. He did not mean that half would be given solely to the church or to strictly religious responsibilities, but rather to duty—the governing of his people and the encouragement of learning, for example, as well as the support of monasteries. But dividing the night into hours was no simple thing. Sun dials did not tell time after sunset and there were no clocks or watches. Alfred turned his inventiveness to the problem and produced a clock, by no means the first in history but the first that his people had seen. It consisted of a set of candles, each twelve inches long and of twelve-penny weight. Each taper, he calculated, should burn for four hours. When one had burned out, the next would be lit. Twelve divisions were marked off on each candle, so that there were divisions into twenty-minute intervals as well as hours. But the practice was not as good as the theory. Variations in air currents affected the speed with which the candles were consumed. So Alfred devised a lantern to hold the burning taper, a wooden-frame shelter with a door and windows of white oxhorn planed so thin as to be not only translucent but transparent. Now he had a reasonably reliable device for measuring the hours.[17]

And what crowded hours they were! The king's light brightened a nation and an age.

91

X

KING'S ENGLISH

*t*he king in his island realm, finds it a lonely task
to mete and dole unequal laws unto [an igno-
rant] race, that hoard, and sleep, and feed, and
know not me...and this gray spirit yearning in desire
to follow knowledge like a sinking star, beyond the ut-
most bound of human thought." In these words Ten-
nyson describes the feelings of a Ulysses returned to
rule a people insular in culture as well as geography.
But the words are almost as applicable to Alfred in
the first half of his reign as to the king of Ithaca as
imagined by the British laureate. In the ninth century
the Vikings had destroyed so many centers of learning and the energies of the Anglo-Saxons had been so
absorbed by defensive war against them, that the cultural retreat from the Golden Age of the seventh and
eighth centuries had been turned into a rout. In
that age a great school in Kent had drawn scholars
from Ireland as well as all parts of England, the Venerable Bede in Northumbria had written in Latin his
monumental *Ecclesiastical History,* and also in the
north the Abbey of Lindisfarne had brought forth
one of the handsomest illuminated texts the world has

ever known, while Charlemagne, seeking to raise the
cultural level of his court and empire, had enticed Alcuin from the headship of a famous school at York.
As we have seen, Alfred himself is witness to the fact
that when he came to the throne in 871 there were
very few churchmen north of the Humber who could
understand the rituals that they performed by rote,
even fewer south of that river, and none south of the
Thames. Most of the earls, many of whom sat as
judges, could not even read English. For Alfred—a
lover of books from a family that revered learning, a
man of such insatiable intellectual curiosity that he
wrote, "The worst thing of all is ignorance"—the environment of ninth century England must have been a
lonely one.

But Alfred's concern was not primarily selfish. He
wanted learning to help him guide his people and he
wanted the people themselves to have education for
self-guidance. Alfred looked back with longing to the
Anglo-Saxon Golden Age. His desire to obtain learning for himself and his people is reminiscent of Charlemagne and, like the Holy Roman Emperor, he
imported scholars to direct his cultural revolution.
But, unlike the great Frankish ruler, Alfred was himself to be the chief intellectual force in his people's
cultural progress. For Charlemagne came too late to
books. When he had mastered an empire, he could
not take knowledge for his province. Contrary to common assumption, the emperor could write in more
than one language and was a keen student, but, unlike Alfred, he never made original contributions to
scholarship.

Alfred was an equally assiduous student and an ex-
traordinarily gifted one. Before undertaking to instruct his people he began to amend his own
education. Though Mercia had declined severely from
days of glory, it still had a few scholars with more
learning than the churchmen of Wessex. Notable, perhaps more because of the lack of competition than because of any great excellence in scholarship, were
Plegmund, archbishop of Canterbury, and two Mer-

cian priests, Athelstan and Werwulf. Alfred invited them to court, made them his teachers, and "exalted them with many honors." Another Mercian scholar, Werefirth, bishop of Worcester, also one of the king's teachers, was persuaded by him to translate the *Dialogues* of Pope Gregory from Latin into Saxon. Night and day, almost any time the king was awake and not busied with the affairs of the kingdom, he had one of these men read to him from Latin works, translating and explaining as they went. Before long he knew the contents of every book obtainable in England.[1]

Alfred's appetite for learning was not satisfied. He turned to the continent in search of teachers. At that time the Abbey of Saint-Bertin, at Saint-Omer, in the Pas-de-Calais, was a great European center of learning and a priest named Grimbald was one of its most respected scholars. Alfred wrote to Fulk, France's proud archbishop of Reims, requesting Grimbald's services at the English court. He softened the request by sending the archbishop some English hounds which the prelate acknowledged would help protect him from "the fury of wolves, of which, among other scourges brought on us by just judgment of God, our country is full." But, whether he feared that Alfred was equating English hounds with a French priest in bizarre barter or he himself simply could not resist the opportunity to lecture a Saxon king, Fulk replied in a manner that showed little respect for royal dignity. He expressed the hope that Alfred, with "diligence and industry," would repair the damages to the English church from "heathen invasions..., negligence of the higher clergy and the ignorance of those under their rule." He also insisted that the priest be consecrated a bishop before leaving France and that an English escort of nobles, bishops, deacons, and priests be provided for him on his journey across the channel. Furthermore, King Alfred was enjoined to guard this French priest well from the "barbaric ferocity" of any of his English subjects.[2]

Alfred's reply to the archbishop is not known. But Grimbald entered the English king's service without

being consecrated a bishop. When Alfred, impressed
by his abilities, sought to reward his services with pro-
motion, Grimbald declined. With a humility that
matched his former lord's arrogance, he asked only
the privilege of continuing his work of scholarship
and teaching.

Another continental scholar whose services Alfred
obtained was John the Old Saxon, a German priest.
Alfred had special plans for him, making him abbot
of a new monastery which the king had built at Athelney. In the bleak days when his island hideout had
been his only kingdom, Alfred had been sustained in
part by a sense of responsibility, in part by pride
(personal, family, national), but also by a strong religious faith that drew strength from a sense of com-
munion with nature. There had been anxious days at
Athelney, but it was there also that the king had
found a peace independent of external circumstance.
It was his hope that other men would find the same
thing in this place. Even the bridge that Alfred constructed to link Athelney with the outer world was no
ordinary structure but a beautiful span between two
towers, one of which was distinguished by an architectural elegance to which most Englishmen were unac-
customed.

Unfortunately, not all men found at Athelney what
Alfred did. French and German priests quarreled bit-
terly, living in close quarters in that isolated place. Re-
bellious French priests hired two French servants of
the house to kill their German abbot while he knelt
alone in nightly prayer. Hearing their footsteps behind his back, John suddenly wheeled upon them
shouting "Devils!" as he landed heavy blows. The
would-be assassins fled, leaving John on the floor in
his own blood. Brought by the shouts and noise of
scuffling, honest priests arrived in time to save his
life.[3]

Asser was a priest of St. David's, in Pembrokeshire.
Hard pressed by repeated Viking attacks, rulers of the
various southern kingdoms of Wales had become vassals of Alfred to obtain his protection. Among these

petty kings was Hyfaild, whose kingdom of Dyfed included St. David's. He had plundered the estates of
this religious community, driving off its bishop, one of
Asser's kinsmen. Asser himself was now under Hyfaild's threat. When invited to court by Alfred, the
Welsh priest must have been delighted by the opportunity to make friends with his persecutor's overlord.

Alfred first invited Asser to visit him at the royal
manor of Dene, near Eastbourne in Sussex. The
Welshman has given us a detailed account of what ensued.[4] The king received him kindly and the two were
soon in pleasant, informal conversation. In the midst
of their talk, Alfred turned to the scholar with a new
eagerness. "Come, devote yourself to my service and
become my friend. I shall give you in my dominions
more than the equivalent of all you leave behind west
of the Severn."

Asser, by his own account, was not overawed. He
replied: "I cannot incautiously and rashly promise
such things. It seems to me unjust that I should leave
those sacred places in which I was bred, educated,
and tonsured"—significantly, the Saxon word which
Asser used also meant *crowned*—"and at last ordained, for the sake of any earthly honor and power,
unless by compulsion."

Alfred did not give up. "If you can't accede to this,
at least let me have your service in part. Spend six
months of the year with me, and the other six in
Wales."

"I can't even promise that easily or hastily," said Asser, "without the advice of my friends."

The king persisted good-humoredly.

At length Asser promised: "If my life is spared, I
shall return to you after six months with a reply that
should be agreeable to you as well as advantageous to
me and mine."

Three days later, Asser parted from Alfred and
rode back toward his country. But he had gone only
as far as Winchester when he was stricken with a fever
that sent him to bed for twelve months and a week.
When the time came for the scholar's return to

Alfred's court, he was, of course, unable to go. When
Asser did not appear, Alfred sent a messenger to find
out why. The Welshman sent the king a report of his
illness and the word, "If I recover from my infirmity I
will fulfill what I promised."

When the priest's illness left him a little more than
six months later, with his friends urging him to serve
the king for the benefit of St. David's, Asser joined
the court. He promised to serve Alfred on the condition that he should remain with him six months of
each year, either continuously, or alternately three
months in England and three in Wales.

The Welshman soon settled into a routine of daily
readings to Alfred from Latin works. Despite his
heavy schedule of official duties, Alfred found time to
read in English and to be read to from Latin during
the day as well as each evening. The king, grateful for
the chance to discuss books with this scholar, showered him with daily gifts. Asser was quite pleased until, when the first six-month period was at an end,
Alfred begged him to stay on. Day after day, Asser
asked to leave. Always, the king pled with him to remain a little longer. At twilight on Christmas Eve, Asser was so depressed by homesickness that he resolved
to demand release. At that time, Alfred sent for him.
The king was waiting with Christmas gifts. He handed
Asser two letters listing properties which henceforward would belong to this priest and presented him
also a silken cloak of great value and a load of incense
so heavy that only a strong man could carry it. "I do
not give you these trifling gifts because I am unwilling
hereafter to give you greater," Alfred said. Asser was
overwhelmed by the richness of these presents and
the promise of more valuable ones to come.

When he returned to St. David's, he had been at
court eight months.

After an interval Asser was back at court. A strong
friendship had developed between sovereign and
priest, and Asser apparently enjoyed as much as
Alfred the conversation about history, literature, and
philosophy. One day's talk was to impress the Welsh-

man so vividly that he recalled the exact date years later and recorded the details with pride-sharpened
memory.[5] The occasion was St. Martin's Day, November 14, 887. Asser relates:

"We were both of us sitting in the king's chamber,
talking on all kinds of subjects as usual, and it happened that I read to him a quotation out of a certain
book. He heard it attentively with both his ears, and
addressed me with a thoughtful mind, showing me at
the same moment a book which he carried in his bos-
om, and in which were written the daily courses and
psalms and prayers which he had read in his youth.
He asked me to write the same quotation in that
book. . . .

"Perceiving his ingenuous behevolence and devout
desire of studying the words of divine wisdom, I gave,
though in secret, boundless thanks to Almighty God,
who had implanted such a love of wisdom in the
king's heart.

"But I could not find in that book any empty space
in which to write the quotation, because it was already
full of various matters. So I made a little delay, chiefly
that I might stir up the bright intellect of the king to
a higher acquaintance with the divine testimonies."

"Make haste!" Alfred urged. "Write it quickly!"

"Are you willing," asked Asser, "that I should write
this quotation on a separate sheet? It's possible that
we shall find other extracts that please you, and if
that happens we shall be glad that we have kept them
separately."

"Your plan is good," Alfred agreed.

Asser tells us:

"I gladly made haste to get ready a sheet, in the beginning of which I wrote what he bade me. And on
that same day I wrote on it, as I had anticipated, no
less than three other quotations which pleased him, so
that the sheet became full. . . . Thus, like a productive
bee, he flew here and there, asking questions as he
went, until he had eagerly and unceasingly collected
many various flowers of divine Scripture, with which
he thickly stored the cells of his mind.

"Now, when that first quotation was copied he was eager at once to read [in Latin] and to interpret in Saxon, and then to teach others...."

Asser was astonished that Alfred "began, on one and the same day, to read and interpret." He tells us:

"The king, inspired by God, began to study the rudiments of divine Scripture on the sacred solemnity of St. Martin, and he continued to cull the flowers collected by certain masters, and to reduce them into the form of one book..., although mixed with one another, until it became almost as large as a psalter. This book he called his *Enchridion*, or handbook, because he carefully kept it *at hand* day and night, and found in it, as he told me, no small consolation."

So Alfred became, in one day, translator and anthologist. His handbook has disappeared, although there is a possibility that it was read and quoted as late as the twelfth century. But other books translated and compiled by Alfred remain, and from the preface to one of them we learn of the great design which he conceived. The king translated into West Saxon, or Old English, Saint Gregory's *Pastoral Care*, a Latin classic of idealistic admonition and practical advice for bishops, sending to each see a copy prefaced with a message to the particular bishop:

"It has very often come into my mind, what wise men there formerly were throughout England, both of sacred and secular orders; and what happy times there were then throughout England, and how the kings who had power over the nation in those days obeyed God and his ministers. And they preserved peace, morality, and order at home, and at the same time enlarged their territory abroad. And how they prospered with war and with wisdom. And also the sacred orders—how zealous they were both in teaching and learning, and in all the services they owed to God. And how foreigners came to this land in search of wisdom and instruction, and how we should now have to get them from abroad if we should have them."[6]

Then followed the famous words which we have already quoted in another context:

"So general was [learning's] decay in England that there were very few on this side of the Humber who could understand their rituals in English, or translate a letter from Latin into English; and I believe that there were not many beyond the Humber. There were so few of them that I cannot remember a single one south of the Thames when I came to the throne. Thanks be to God Almighty that we have any teachers among us now.

"And therefore I direct you to do as I believe you are willing, to disengage yourself from worldly matters as often as you can, that you may apply the wisdom which God has given you whenever you can. Consider what punishments would come upon us on account of this world, if we neither loved [wisdom] ourselves nor enabled other men to obtain it: we should love only the name of Christian and very few of the virtues.

"When I considered all this, I remembered also how I saw, before all the ravaging and burning, how the churches throughout the whole of England stood filled with treasures and books, and there was also a great multitude of God's servants, but they had very little knowledge of the books, for they could not understand anything in them, because they were not written in their own language. As if they had said: 'Our forefathers, who formerly held these places, loved wisdom, and through it they obtained wealth and bequeathed it to us. In this we can still see their tracks, but we cannot follow them, and therefore we have lost both the wealth and the wisdom because we would not incline our hearts after their example.' "

Alfred continued:

When I remembered all this, I wondered extremely that the good and wise men who were formerly all over England, and had perfectly learnt all the books, did not wish to translate them into their own language. But again I soon answered myself and said: "They did not think that men would ever be so careless, and that learning would so decay; through that hope they abstained from . . . [the task], and they wished that the wisdom in this land might increase with our knowledge of languages. Then I remembered how the law was first known in Hebrew, and again, when the Greeks had learnt it, they translated the whole of it into their own language, and all other books besides. And again the Romans, when they had learnt it, they translated the whole of it through learned interpreters into their own language. And also all other Christian nations translated a part of them into their own languages.

Therefore it seems better to me, if you think so, for us also to translate some books which are most needful for all men to know into the language which we can all understand, and I or you to do as we very easily can if we have tranquillity enough, that is that all the youth now in England of free men, who have the ability to devote themselves to it, be set to learn as long as they are not fit for any other occupation, until they are well able to read English writing: and let those be afterwards taught more in the Latin language who are to continue learning and be promoted to a higher rank.

When I remembered how the knowledge of Latin had formerly decayed throughout England, and yet many could read English writing, I began, among other various and manifold troubles of this kingdom, to translate into English the book which is called in Latin *Pastoralis*, and in English *Shepherd's Book*, sometimes word by word and sometimes according to the sense, as I had learnt it from Plegmund my archbishop, and Asser my bishop, and Grimbold my mass-priest, and John my mass-priest. And when I had learnt it as I could best understand it, and as I could most clearly interpret it, I translated it into English; and I will send a copy to every bishopric in my kingdom.[7]

Alfred's preface is notable in several respects. It announces his determination to restore learning to England by a threefold process: stimulating the clergy to scholarly endeavor in learning and teaching, translating the books "which are most needful for all men to know into the language which we can all understand," and teaching the youth of England to read their native language.

Though Alfred greeted each recipient bishop "with words loving and friendly" and softened his admonitions with "it seems better to me, if you think so," his tact did not blur the fact that he was serving notice on a negligent clergy that it must return to productive scholarship. Viking raids on the monasteries admittedly were more than distracting but, as the king pointed out in his preface, the decline in learning had set in before the Danish attacks attained great frequency and high intensity. Alfred was informing the bishops that the clergy, next to the king himself, must bear the heavy load of leadership in uplifting the people ethically and educationally. As he said on another occasion, priests were among the tools needed by a king if he was to serve his people well.

In attempting to translate into English "the books most needful for all men to know" Alfred was taking on a gargantuan task. He would have the aid of scholars, but this king, so lately come to Latin and more busily involved than any of his predecessors in every constructive activity of his people, would himself assume the major burden of translation and interpretation. He would provide a guide book for ecclesiastics, a history of Britain, a history of the world, a geography of Europe, a collection of stories, a book of classical philosophy and a volume of Christian philosophy. In some cases, notably in geography, he would make important contributions through original research. He had the sophistication to decide that, though sometimes he would render "word for word," at other times he would translate "sense for sense." Indeed, he would make some old classics so vivid for his fellow Englishmen by substituting his own figures of speech for the originals that he would be as much co-author as translator. He would for the first time make English a literary language, bending and molding it to express abstractions and subtleties that had never before been expressed in that tongue. Almost single-handedly and within a decade he would force English through a process of maturation ordinarily achieved by a language only through several generations of evolution helped along by many minds. And all this he had the boldness to attempt, though suffering from a chronic illness, while welding one kingdom out of many, supervising all the arts of peace, and defending his island realm against the greatest sea warriors in the world.

Alfred intended his translation of Gregory's *Pastoral Care* to be an instrument of reform as well as of learning. His sense of the urgent need for reform among the clergy was implicit in his admonition to the bishops to "disengage [themselves] from worldy matters" as often as they could to devote themselves to the acquisition and application of wisdom. Alfred's love of beautiful books, dating from his childhood, may have caused him to take care to make copies of the new translation esthetically pleasing. But it was undoubtedly his knowledge of the ninth century Anglo-Saxon clergy's respect for material things that caused him to call attention to the fact that the book-marker placed in the volume sent to each see was worth fifty mancuses—the value of three hundred sheep. A beautiful gem found in 1693 near the site of Athelney Abbey was long thought to be the jeweled tip of one of these bookmarkers, probably rods that also doubled as pointers. More recent scholarship suggests that the jewel may have been used as a paperweight to hold open the heavy vellum leaves. Fashioned of pure gold, colored stones, and enamel mosaic, this exquisite work of art, now known as Alfred's jewel, depicts an enthroned figure with a scepter in each hand and bears the engraved words AELFRED MEC HEHT GEWYRCAN: "Alfred had me made."[8]

The manual which Alfred translated for the guidance of the clergy had been brought to England by St. Augustine in 596 when he came to convert the Saxons. In the eighth century the great Alcuin had advised one of his successors in York: "Wherever you go, let the Pastoral Book of Saint Gregory go with you." The veneration in which the Anglo-Saxons held St. Gregory was perhaps enhanced by the well-known story of his exclaiming, on being told that some golden-haired slaves in a Roman market were Angles: "That is a good name for them for they have angelic faces. They must become not Angles but Angels."

The book was for several reasons a good choice to inaugurate Alfred's program of translations. The king believed improvement and stimulation of the clergy to be essential to his educational program. The *Pastoral Care* would be a guide to ecclesiastics in personal conduct, administration and teaching. Werferth's translation of Gregory's *Dialogues*, instigated by Alfred, had paved the way for another work by the same author. Furthermore, much of Gregory's practical advice was such as to be valuable to civilian as well as ecclesiastical administrators.

As might be expected, Alfred's *Pastoral Care* is nearer to the Latin original than any of his later translations. He gained skill and confidence with each new work and consequently translated more and more "sense for sense," all the while making English prose an increasingly flexible medium.

But the closeness of Alfred's translation to the original Latin of Gregory's work should not be exaggerated, as it too often has been. Henry Sweet noted in 1871:

> ...there seems to be no attempt to engraft Latin idioms on the English version: the foreign influence is only indirect, chiefly showing itself in the occasional clumsiness that results from the difficulty of expressing and defining abstract ideas in a language unused to theological and metaphysical subtleties.[9]

Many of Alfred's problems as translator were rooted in the state of Old English at the time that he was working to make it a literary language. A language of ordinary speech and of poetry, it characteristically placed clauses, phrases, or words in succession without the use of coordinating or subordinating connectives. This parataxis led to monotony when Alfred sought to express subtle relationships and complex abstractions. Pleonasms, frequent in some English dialects today ("The man he said so"), are numerous. So are repetitions reminiscent of the efforts of a schoolmaster to drill ideas into the heads of his pupils. As Sweet has said: "It is evident that the sole object of the translator was to reproduce the sense of the original in such a way as to be intelligible to an unlearned Englishman of the ninth century."[10] Old English prose would be a more flexible medium in the tenth century, but largely because of Alfred's efforts.

Far more notable than Alfred's occasional awkwardness, however, is his general facility in this first translation. He has succeeded remarkably well in making a Latin classic intelligible and readable for his English audience and in doing so has boldly departed from Latin syntax. Indeed, Alfred's prose was much farther removed from a slavish dependence on Roman forms than that of so respected an English stylist as John Dryden eight centuries later. Three distinguished German linguists of the nineteenth century, Gustav Wack, Albert Dewitz, and J. E. Wulfing, demonstrated through detailed analysis Alfred's independence of Latin syntax. In the twentieth century, a Frenchman, Paul Bacquet, and an American, William Brown, Jr., have convincingly revealed the essentially idiomatic character of the king's translation. Though echoing Sweet's statement that the *Pastoral Care* is the closest to its Latin source of any of Alfred's renderings, Brown concludes:

"Alfred translates word by word infrequently. His usual practice is dissolving the long Latin sentences, dense with nouns and participles, into combinations of short clauses that may preserve little more than Gregory's thesis. . . . he has culled the sense while rejecting both the complicated rhetoric and syntax that support it."[11]

Indeed, Alfred's great accomplishment may be marred by even fewer faults than students have commonly supposed. Perhaps a reassessment is needed of the significance of both pleonasms and parataxis in his writing. Pleonasms are not always unforgiveable redundancies. They have added to the rhythmic force of numerous English ballads. There spring to mind such unsophisticated examples as the opening lines of "Dives and Lazarus": "And it fell out upon a day, Rich *Dives he* made a feast. . . ." or the words of "The Three Ravens":

"Down in yonder greene field,
    "There lies a knight slain under his shield.

"*His hounds they* lie down at his feet,
    "So well they can their master keep.

"*His hawks they* fly so eagerly,
    "There's no fowl dare him come nigh."

In the foregoing lines, the inexact rhyme is far more naive than the use of pleonasms, which actually enhances the plaintive effect. One thinks, too, of the use of the same device in the old Scottish ballad "Hind Horn" and in "The Twa Sisters." The reader may readily think of many examples from popular balladry, some of much more recent origin than the ones discussed here.

A more sophisticated, carefully calculated use of the device was made by Rudyard Kipling in "The Liner She's a Lady," and especially in "Tomlinson" in such lines as:

"*The Wind* that blows between the Worlds, *it* nipped him to the bone,

"And he yearned to the flare of Hell-gate there as the light of his own hearth-stone.

"The *Devil he* sat behind the bars, when the desperate legion drew,

"But he caught the hasting Tomlinson and would not let him through."

And in the especially memorable:

"The *Devil he* blew on a brandered soul and set it aside to cool:"

Alfred's pleonasm is admittedly awkward in such expressions as: "Therefore it is again said in the book of Solomon that we call the Song of Songs, it is said: . . . ."

But is there no compensation at all when the terse Latin "Magnus quippe susceptae Ecclesias cononus" becomes "Wietoddice se *maera landbegaega, daet waes sanctus Paulus*, he underfeng pa holgen gesomnunga to plantinanne & to ymbhweorfanne"? (Truly *the great husbandman, that is Saint Paul, he* undertook to plant and to tend the holy assembly.) To change Lincoln's

"Four score and seven years ago our fathers brought forth on this continent a new nation" to "Eighty-seven years ago our fathers created a nation" is to gain in terseness at the expense of rhythm. While lacking the majestic cadence of Lincoln's prose, some of Alfred's pleonasms are not entirely without charm.

That other bugaboo of Alfred's translation, parataxis, does not rear its primitive head in Alfred's *Pastoral Care* nearly so often as many nonreaders of the work suppose. Culling the text with care, Brown found seven examples. Not all of these are egregious, or even awkward. S. O. Andrew, in his *Syntax and Style in Old English*, distinguishes between parataxis as a fault of style and parataxis as an effective rhetorical device.[12] The first is a jerry-built construction whose lack of grammatical subordination is only too painfully apparent. An example often cited is the *Anglo-Saxon Chronicle*'s entry for 757 (755 by one calculation), in which the exciting story of Cynewulf's assassination in his mistress's bower is tediously told in a string of phrases and clauses begging for subordinating connectives. The king's English is better. Alfred sometimes uses rhetorical parataxis with the skill of the Saxon versifiers who produced *Beowulf*. For example, there is eloquence in his rendering: "They sell for too small a price that with which they could buy the kingdom of heaven: they sell it for the praise of men."

Alfred doubtless found in Gregory's "thought hoard" much to fit his own needs. Almost certainly, the king was reminded of his days at Athelney, as well as of his initial reluctance to accept the throne, when he translated the words:

> Often a man is subjected to the instruction of adversity. . . . But although schooled and taught by adversity, soon, if he attain to power, through the homage of the people he becomes proud and accustomed to presumption—as King Saul at first declined the throne, and deemed himself quite unworthy of it, but as soon as he obtained the rule of the kingdom, he became proud.[13]

In some of Alfred's original comments inserted into other translations we find expressed a dread of *hubris*

that seems to be more than a conventional warning
against pride. Alfred evidently resolved that he would
not become "accustomed to presumption." In the *Pastoral Care*, Alfred also translates:

> Often when anyone happens to do anything famous
> and wonderful, and those who are under him, admiring it, praise him, he is puffed up in spirit, and completely calls down on himself the full ire of his Judge,
> although he does not show his pride in bad deeds.[14]

Alfred, who had been tempted to pursue his own
intellectual development without assuming the burden
of ruling a beleaguered people, must have been a little introspective when he translated Gregory's stricture against those who avoid positions of responsibility
for which they are well qualified. "If, when such power is offered them, they refuse it, it often happens
that they are deprived of the gifts which God bestowed on them for the sake of many men, not of
them alone."[15]

This book, which Alfred regarded so greatly, contained words of advice to bishops that were especially
applicable to kings, among them:

> It is very necessary for the ruler to be zealously vigilant and careful, lest the desire of popularity overcome
> him.[16]

> It also often happens that, when [the ruler] reproves
> his subjects too excessively, his words become perverted to useless loquacity.[17]

For all its interest, however, Alfred's translation of
Gregory's *Pastoral Care* can give little sure evidence of
Alfred's own thoughts. The fact that a man is enthusiastic about a book does not automatically justify the
assumption that he agrees with every statement in it,
or even that he would place the author's emphasis on
everything with which he does agree. Particular interest, therefore, attaches to what is believed to be
Alfred's next work, his editorial direction and perhaps
co-authorship of Orosius' *Historia Adversum Paganos*
(*History Against the Pagans*), in which he and his co-
workers not only are especially free in substituting

109

their own figures of speech for the author's, and in
omitting parts of the original text, but also interpolate
passages of their own composition, including an entire
chapter based on the King's own research that is an
important contribution to knowledge.

Paulus Orosius was a fifth century Spanish theolo-
gian and historian whose *Historia* enjoyed more prestige in Medieval Europe than any comparable work.
Written principally to refute the pagan claim that
more disasters had befallen the Roman Empire since
the coming of Christianity than before, the book nec-
essarily emphasizes the calamities that befell pre-Chris-
tian Rome. But since so much of man's story has been
written in blood—"Happy nations have no history"—
the long tale of disasters was the most comprehensive
record of Western civilization available to medieval
man. After the invention of the printing press, it was
one of the first books chosen for reproduction by the
revolutionary new method. Many printed editions followed the first, brought out in Germany in 1471.[18]
The popularity of the book in the ninth century was
such that the identity of the author and work had
merged, as attested by the first sentence of Alfred's
translation: "Here begins the book which men call
Orosius."

Though weakened by bias and misinformation,
Orosius' work made a valuable contribution to medieval culture. He had studied under two internationally
famous scholars, Saint Augustine, bishop of Hippo
Regius, in Africa, and Saint Jerome in Palestine, both
of whom paid high tribute to his abilities. Nevertheless Alfred was not awed by Orosius' reputation. He
and his aids drastically edited the *Historia* in ways that
tremendously increased the usefulness and readability
of the work. They abridged and reorganized the sev-
en volumes of the Latin original to make only six volumes in the Anglo-Saxon version, even with the
addition of Alfred's new essays, reducing by half Orosius' two hundred chapters. The Spanish historian's
work extended chronologically from Creation through
the adventures of Adam and his descendants to the

year 409. The Anglo-Saxons summarily deleted Orosius' introductory chapter and reduced to a single
paragraph his account of the Creation and all subsequent happenings down to the reign of Ninus, king of
Assyria. They added accounts of the geography, life,
and customs of Europe in their own day. They also
omitted the last four chapters (21-24) of the fifth
book and chapters 1, 2, 3, 5, 8, 9, 11, 12, 13, and 14
of the sixth, abridging some of the remaining chapters. Orosius' seventh book, generally abridged and
minus the last three chapters, is the sixth book of
Alfred's work.

Alfred has not given us a dismembered corpse, but
a coordinated living work. Its unity, suggested by the
Anglo-Saxon table of contents (the Latin original had
none), is confirmed by examination of the text. As reconstructed by the Englishmen, Book I gives a geography of the world as then known to the scholars of
Western Europe plus material gained from the king's
interviews with mariners, together with a summary of
"world" history from earliest times to the founding of
Rome. Book II tells of the Babylonian, Greek, Egyp-
tian, and Roman empires, with the emphasis on Roman history down to the invasion of the city by the
Gauls. Book III deals chronologically with the wars of
the Romans, Carthaginians, Persians, Gauls, and other
Mediterranean peoples, concluding with the slaying of
Seleucus by Ptolemy. Book IV continues the story of
Rome from the Pyrrhic War to the destruction of Carthage. Book V covers Mediterranean history from the
taking of Corinth to the birth of Christ. Book VI sum-
marizes "world" history and carries the Roman story
forward from the accession of Tiberius Caesar to the
sacking of the city by Alaric the Goth. Before Alfred
and his aids completed their translation of Orosius, he
learned a good deal of history, becoming acquainted
with a half dozen empires and with such men as De-
mosthenes, Alexander, Hannibal, Darius, Xerxes, Julius Caesar, Marcus Antoninus, and Augustus. Later
we have direct evidence that Alfred studied Orosius in
part with an eye toward improving the military and

naval strategy with which he would defend his kingdom. Surely the English king, whose predilection was
for the arts of peace, must also have gained ideas of
statecraft. He undoubtedly found figures outside the
Anglo-Saxon kingdom, the Danelaw, and the Kingdom of the Franks by whom he could measure his at-
tainments and his aspirations. Above all, like his trips
to Rome in childhood, the study of *Orosius* opened
for Alfred a door upon the great world.

Though idiosyncracies of syntax and vocabulary
mark the manuscript as the work of several writers,
Alfred may well have been one of these as well as the
general sponsor, planner, and supervisor of the work.

It may be accurate to picture Alfred, brows knitted,
poring over the Latin text in purse-lipped concentration. It undoubtedly is accurate to picture him in earnest consultation with clerical scholars on points that
puzzled him. But we very likely stray from the truth
when we visualize him bent over a copy desk tran-
scribing the English words of his portions of the
translation. He probably sat, glancing now and then
from the Latin text to his own notes, as he dictated to
a secretary.

Ann Kirkman has convincingly presented her theory that Alfred dictated his translations of the *Orosius*
to an amanuensis who misunderstood many of the
foreign names.[19] She suggests that the king himself
did not fully understand the Roman system of personal names, citing examples of metathesis and confusion
of inflexional suffixation.

Far more impressive than any errors, however, are
the ways in which Alfred's translation is superior to
the original *Orosius*, as a work designed specifically
for English readers and as a universal history. Some
of the ways in which Alfred and his aids Englished his
work are amusing as well as effective. In Chapter VII
of Book III, where the English author tells how Philip
of Macedon took to the sea to satisfy his people's hunger for booty, the English writer assures relevancy to
his audience by saying succinctly, "He gathered ships
and they became Vikings." When he tells in Chapter

IV of Book IV about a *virgo Vestalia*, or Vestal virgin, who was hanged for a sexual offense, he conveys the proper sense of self-desecration and horror by calling her a "nun."

The value of the work both to the king's contemporary English audience and to scholars everywhere through succeeding generations is enhanced most of all by his essay on the geography of Europe. If Alfred had never performed any service but the writing or coordination of this essay he would have earned a place in history. The king accepts in general Orosius' picture of the world as consisting principally of three continents—Asia, Africa, and Europe—and the seas surrounding them. West of Europe were the British Isles and much farther west was "that outmost land called Thule," which is believed to be Iceland. Alfred's great contribution was his recognition of the inadequacy of the Spanish scholar's accounts of central and northern Europe and his effectiveness in remedying these deficiencies. Many historians have echoed Sir Frank Stenton's appraisal of Alfred's work:

> No one before him had attempted such a survey. As a piece of systematic geography it stands alone in the Dark Ages, and at most disputable points its accuracy has been confirmed by modern research.[20]

Alfred made the greatest contribution to European geography in four hundred years. Though Norse explorations would extend to America in the eleventh century, there was to be no comparable European contribution to systematic geography for at least the next three centuries. And that possible contender, Marco Polo's account of his journeying in Asia, was actually more of a travel book than a geography. For organized geographical reporting such as Alfred provided, we must turn either to four Arabians, Abu Zaid, al-Masudi, Istakhri, and Idrisi, or wait until the fifteenth century activities of Prince Henry the Navigator. Among Alfred's other achievements, as Preston E. James points out, he "first reduced to writing the discoveries of the earliest polar explorer and intro-

duced to literature the midnight sun of the arctic
summer."[21]

Both of these phenomena appear in the king's account of the historic voyages of discovery by Ohthere,
a rich landholder in northern Norway. Ohthere was a
keen observer as well as a bold mariner, and Alfred
had the good judgment to preserve the concrete details that impart the flavor of the Norwegian's own
narrative as well as confirming its authenticity. The
start of the story suggests an interesting possibility:
"Ohthere told his lord, King Alfred, that he lived farthest north of all northmen....He said that, at a certain time, he wished to find out how far the land
reached due north, or whether any man lived north
of the wasteland. So he sailed due north along the
coast, and all the way he had on the starboard the
empty land and on the larboard the open sea." The
reference to King Alfred as Ohthere's lord may indicate that this Norwegian was in the king's employ. As
the context makes it clear that Ohthere had completed
his voyage due north when he was first received at the
English court, there seems no possibility that this particular venture was sponsored by Alfred. But the quotation does raise the possibility that the king employed
him afterward, perhaps on ventures of both mercan-
tile and geographical significance, in the manner of
Portugal's Prince Henry six centuries later. While
Ohthere might have addressed the king as "my lord"
purely as a social convention, there seems no reason
for the king to have called himself Ohthere's lord if
the mariner was not in his service.

The Norseman had sailed round North Cape, Europe's northern-most promotory, and then eastward
and southward into the White Sea. The route, as P. J.
Helm points out, is that followed by the Arctic con-
voys of World War II. From Ohthere Alfred learned
about the lives of the Finns as fishermen, fowlers, and
hunters, and about the people, variously known as
Beormas or Persians, who inhabited the shores of the
White Sea east of the Dwina River. Alfred differenti-
ates between what Ohthere was told by the people

with whom he talked and what he saw for himself.
The distinction between firsthand and secondhand information had been carefully observed by Herodotus, but had been disregarded by historians who succeeded him. Ohthere had continued his voyage partly because of curiosity but also partly to hunt the "horse-whales" for "the good bone in their teeth." These were walrus and the teeth were, of course, the ivory tusks, some of which Ohthere presented to Alfred. Incidentally, Alfred has been cited as the first writer known to have "placed the whale and walrus in the same class of animals."[22] J. A. Giles thought that the king's conclusion in this matter was as worthy of applause as Linnaeus's perception that the whale, despite its fishlike appearance, was a mammal.

Alfred also records information obtained by Ohthere in a voyage down the coast of Norway to Oslo, and in a sea journey from Oslo to southern Denmark. In mentioning Jutland and Zealand, Alfred notes, "The Angles lived in these lands before they came into this country." This reference has long interested historians concerned with the continental origins of England's population.

The king also included in his essay information which he obtained from Ohthere about life in his native Norway. Here we have a picture of the rich Norwegian, with his herd of six hundred reindeer, as well as cows, sheep, hogs, and horses, living a life comparable to that of the cattle barons of the American West. Ohthere clearly was an amphibious success. It is easy to see why Alfred delighted in him.

Another captain whose explorations enriched Alfred's geography was Wulfstan, now sometimes thought to be a Dane but generally considered an Englishman. He sailed from South Denmark to Poland and Estonia. Alfred was fascinated with Wulfstan's revelations concerning the life of the Estonians. They had many towns and in every one there was a king. Of course, this statement might be sailor talk for many villages with a chief in each. Fishing was good and honey was abundant. Only the poor and slaves

drank mead, the traditional beverage of the Anglo-
Saxons. Kings and rich men drank mare's milk, undoubtedly the fermented, brandylike beverage drunk
both in Central Asia and ancient Prussia.[23] There was
also a great deal of fighting, but it is not clear whether Alfred's informant regarded that circumstance as a
drawback or an advantage.

Particularly interesting to Alfred were the funeral
customs of the Estonians. A corpse was always kept
unburied and unburnt in the house of the deceased
for at least a month, longer if the dead man was of a
high social position. The body of a king might be kept
in his house for six months. All the time that the body
remained above ground there was merrymaking with
drinking and sports.

This keeping of the corpses would seem to involve
serious problems. Even kings decay and become offensive. When Charles the Bald died while returning
to France from Italy in 877 he had to be buried far
from home because the coffin bearers refused to endure the stench of putrefaction. Alfred was curious
to know the Estonian solution and astonished when he
heard it. "There is among the Estonions," Wulfstan
told him, "a power of producing cold, and therefore
the dead lie there so long and do not decay. And if
anyone sets two vessels full of ale or water, they cause
one to be frozen whether it be summer or winter."[24] A
mystery, indeed, unless one concludes, as most scholars have, that Wulfstan did not understand that the
inhabitants kept icehouses that furnished sufficient ice
to preserve animals for eating and corpses for burial.
Hakluyt's *Voyages* contained a bit of doggerel written
in Moscow by G. Tuberville in allusion to the practice
of delayed burial among the Russians:

> Perhaps thou musest much, how this may stand with
> reason, That bodies dead can uncorrupt abide so long
> a season! Take this for certain truth: as soon as heat is
> gone The force of cold the body binds as hard as any
> stone, Without offense at all to any living thing; And so
> they lie in perfect state till next return of spring.[25]

What Tuberville lacked in poetic grace, he made up in boldness. His verse was addressed to Edmund Spenser.

No less fascinating to Alfred than the extended wake were the customs observed on the day of burial. On the appointed date, the neighbors of the deceased would divide all his property remaining, after the drinking and the expenditure for celebration, into five or more parts.

> Then they lay the largest part of it within one mile of the town, then another, then the third, till it is all laid within the one mile; and the least part shall be nearest the town in which the dead man lies. All the men who have the swiftest horses in the land shall then be assembled about five or six miles from the property. Then they all race toward the property, and the man who has the fastest horse comes to the first and the largest part, and so each after the other, till it is all taken, and he takes the least part who runs to the property nearest the town. Then each rides away with the property [he has won] and may keep it. Therefore fast horses are there uncommonly dear.
>
> When the dead man's property is thus all spent, they carry him out and burn him with his weapons and clothes. Most commonly they spend all his wealth, with the long lying of the dead within, and what they lay in the way, which those not connected with him race for and take away.[26]

Alfred's anecdotal accounts of the Estonians doubtless diverted his ninth century audience. Scholars of the nineteenth and twentieth centuries have regarded them as "a valuable supplement to the short sketches of aboriginal manners delineated by Caesar and Tacitus."[27]

Though not as entertaining as the narratives of voyages, Alfred's description of Central Europe from the Rhine to the Don and from the Danube to the White Sea shows him at his best as a systematic geographer. Some scholars, while highly praising Alfred's account of this vast territory, have criticized his "mistake" in calling it Germania. But can we say that Alfred was in

error simply because he had extended the label
"Germania" to include much more than Tacitus had
meant by the term more than eight hundred years before? The Germanic peoples themselves had extended
the areas of their habitation and influence since the
days of the Roman historian. The Goths had moved
into ancient Scythia, which today is within the borders
of the Soviet Union. And later, as we have seen, Scandinavians not only moved into Russia but gave it its
name.

Alfred's troubles with the Danes did not keep him
from recognizing them as part of the great Teutonic
family of peoples to which his own West Saxons be-
longed. He gave as much attention to the North
Danes and South Danes as to the Moravians, whose
accomplishments he admired, or to the East Franks,
with whom he had friendly relations, and to the Old
Saxons, whose kinship to the people of Wessex was
remote but recognized.

As R. H. Hodgkin pointed out, Alfred's geographical essay tells us more about Northern Europe than
any other author's work ever had.[28] Moreover, as Jo-
seph Bosworth noted, Alfred's account also furnishes
information obtainable from no other source.[29] He
probably gathered his information from merchants
and mariners, eventually organizing it into a meaningful whole. Part of Alfred's work was republished in
Hakluyt's *Voyages* in the sixteenth century. Scholars of
the English-speaking world have used it ever since.[30]
Their evaluation of Alfred's contribution is equaled by
the estimate of scholars of other nations, notably Ras-
mus Christian Rask, the great Danish philologist and
orientalist; Friedrich Christoph Dahlmann, the illus-
trious German historian of the northern peoples; and
other historians and geographers from Sweden, Denmark and Germany.

By the translation of *Orosius* Alfred increased his
people's knowledge of the great world beyond their
own shores, discouraging geographical parochialism
by reminders that they lived on sea lanes leading to
cultures cherishing values very different from their
own, discouraging temporal provincialism by remind-

ing them that they moved down a road traveled ahead of them by the Ptolemies and Alexander the Great, and well worn by the chariot wheels of the Caesars.

Alfred also took steps to increase his people's knowledge of their own island. He sponsored an Anglo-Saxon translation of the Latin text of Bede's *Historia Ecclesiastica Gentis Anglorum (Ecclesiastical History of the English People)*. The author of the original, known to history as the Venerable Bede, was the foremost Anglo-Latin writer of Northumbria's Golden Age. Given into the care of the famous Wearmouth-Jarrow monastery about 680 A.D. when he was in his seventh year, he spent the rest of his life in that establishment, studying, teaching, and writing. The author of many books circulated widely on the continent for several centuries, he dictated his last work in the final hours of his life in 735. Greatest of all his writings was the *Historia Ecclesiastica*, which has earned him the title "father of English history." So eminent a scholar as Kemp Malone declares: "This work is our primary source of information about the most momentous period in English history: the period of change from barbarism to civilization. In other words, Bede is not only first among English historians in point of time; he is also first in importance."[31]

Bede not only possessed some narrative skill; he was also a conscientious historian who tried, not always successfully but with more success than most of his contemporaries, to separate legend from fact. Furthermore, his warm humanity shines through his writing with peculiar charm. The variety of his interests makes his book a work of secular as well as ecclesiastical history. If *Orosius* was the inevitable choice to give the English a view of world history, Bede was the inevitable choice to tell them the story of their own nation. His prescience had heightened the appropriateness of the choice. The venerable monk of Jarrow was indeed "the first writer to conceive of the English as one people with a single destiny."[32]

Some people have credited Alfred himself with the translation of Bede's classic, but the attribution is doubtful. There are in the work Mercian phrases

119

which the West-Saxon king is not known to have used
elsewhere. Furthermore, keen students of Old English
have called attention to strong similarities of style between the Anglo-Saxon translation of Bede's book and
that of Gregory's *Dialogue*, which was undertaken at
Alfred's request by Werferth, the Mercian bishop.
Scholars generally agree, however, that the *Bede* was
translated about the same time as the *Orosius* and that
Alfred had at least an editorial hand in the work. As
noted by E. Thomson in his preface to his modern
English translation from Alfred's Anglo-Saxon rendering of the *Historia Ecclesiastica*, "the same plan of
selection and condensation" prevails as in the English
king's *Orosius*.[33] Both show the bold hand of one who
carried royal habits into the Republic of Letters.

The Old English translation of Bede's book made
available to literate Englishmen the story of their
country from Julius Caesar's invasion in 55 B.C. to 731
A.D. or, in Bede's words, "this time of peace and tranquility" in which his manuscript was completed. A
Golden Age, indeed, that must have seemed to the
ninth century king of a Viking-harassed land!

So much for the history of England down to 731
A.D. There remained a great gap between that date
and Alfred's own time.

This want was filled in Alfred's reign by the *Anglo-
Saxon Chronicle*. Authorship of these annals has been
attributed to the king, partly on the basis of the closeness of some passages to the wording of sentences in
his translation of Orosius.[34] But leading scholars of the
Chronicle have been quick to point out certain errors
in it that Alfred would not have made, as when his
childhood ceremonial investment as a Roman consul
was mistaken for a consecration as king.[35] Certainly,
while the compilation of the *Chronicle* as a consistent
record began in Alfred's reign, its origins antedate his
lifetime. After irregular entries referring to events in
universal or British history the *Chronicle* becomes in
624 an almost consistent series of annual entries.
There is much internal evidence that the compilers
relied on Bede's *Historica Ecclesiastica*, genealogies,

regnal lists, some northern annals, and earlier annals of the West Saxons. It has been suggested that the compilation of a limited forerunner of the *Chronicle* may have been begun in Ethelwulf's reign and that Alfred simply directed that the work begun under his father be continued in a frame of greater geographical scope.[36] In any event, it is difficult to believe that Alfred, intensely interested in the education of his people and in the preservation of their history, kept hands off a contemporary enterprise so vitally connected with both. Although the king's authorship of the *Chronicle* is highly doubtful, the influence of his proclivity for systemization and enthusiasm for dissemination seems evident. The seven surviving manuscripts of the *Chronicle*, which vary in some particulars, are today our greatest single source for Anglo-Saxon history, not only through the reign of Alfred but even into the days of Norman Rule.

Alfred was not content to view history as a continuous pageant. It was not enough to know that generations of men were in a procession down the long sweep of the centuries. What was the significance of their journey? Or of any individual's journey? Alfred's "desire to know" led him to philosophy. It was inevitable, given the strength of the king's pedagogic impulse, that his more reflective subjects would be led to the same study.

Alfred was strongly drawn to the *Consolations of Philosophy* by Boethius. *De Consolatione Philosophiae* was the chief work through which a portion of the philosophical learning of Greece and Rome was transmitted to medieval Europe.[37] Alfred became the first person to translate the book into English, and his rendering remains today one of the three most famous translations of it in the language. It is also generally regarded as the most eloquent of the three, despite the fact that one of the others was by no less a lord of language than Geoffrey Chaucer. The king's version is far superior to the third translation, interestingly enough the work of one of Alfred's descendants, Queen Elizabeth I.

Scholars have sometimes noted Alfred's apparent
affinity for the fifth century Roman whose master-
piece he translated. This sympathy may have resulted
in part from similar circumstances in their lives. Both
were of royal blood; both held high office, dividing
their time between political and scholarly projects;
and both were forced to become fugitives. But here
the parallel ends. Alfred, as we know, emerged from
the swamps of Athelney to rule his kingdom. The
Consolations of Philosophy was composed by Boethius
while he sat in prison awaiting his execution. But
there is an intellectual kinship not dependent on the
practical circumstances of individual lives. The English king was a remarkably sane person, exceptionally
free of most superstitions in an especially superstitious
age. He had a marked genius for clarification in a
time when many scholars had a conspicuous talent for
obfuscation. After surveying European thought from
the third century through the fifteenth, Bertrand
Russell concluded that Boethius was freer of "superstition and fanaticism" than any other eminent thinker
within that period of twelve centuries. Lord Russell
added: "He would have been remarkable in any age;
in the age in which he lived, he is utterly amazing."[38]

The Alfred who translated Boethius was far more
sophisticated than the Alfred who commissioned the
translation of Gregory's *Dialogues*, a book of morals
whose appeal sometimes seems directed mainly to the
naive. In studying Boethius the king also moved beyond his *Pastoral Care*, a guide to conduct and practical
administration, into the rarefied realms of metaphys-
ics. Boethius was a Neo-Platonist, and through his
book Alfred learned about the Platonic idea—the un-
concretized essence that is the ultimate reality. A subtle concept for the ninth century English king to
master! A remarkably subtle one for him to express in
the infant prose of his people! And he must deal, also, with a concept of time universal that dwarfed even
the sweep of twenty-eight centuries in Orosius.

But, though the intellectual leap demanded of
Alfred was a great and bold one, his cultural heritage

had prepared him better for it than is often supposed.
He was reared in a family even more deeply imbued
with Christian teaching than most royal households of
the ninth century. The idea that the ultimate reality
lay in the unseen was sufficiently familiar to Alfred to
keep him from rejecting outright the Platonic notion
of transcendent entity. St. Paul's image of life as "seen
through a glass darkly" prepared the king's understanding for reception of an epistemology inspired by
Plato's imagery of the cave. Christianity, too, had told
him of a time span in which a single lifetime was as
the twinkling of an eye. And there was in his Anglo-
Saxon heritage one of man's most memorable images
of the brevity of human life in the immensity of
eternity. The quotation, a model for Alfred in the
concrete presentation of the abstract, is preserved in
Bede's *Ecclesiastical History.* Telling of the conversion
to Christianity of Northumbria's King Edwin in 627,
Bede relates the story of a council at which the chief
priest, Coifi, admitted to his sovereign that the old religion of the Saxon forefathers seemed to have little
efficacy. Arguing that Christianity might offer more
hope, another councillor eloquently said:

> "O king, this present life of men on earth appears to
> me, in comparison with the time that is unknown to us,
> as if you were sitting at a banquet with your chief men
> and thanes, in winter tide, and a fire were kindled, and
> your hall warmed, and it rained and snowed, and
> stormed without; and as if then came a sparrow and
> quickly flew through the house; and came in through
> one door, and went out through another. Lo! in the
> time that he is within he is not touched by the storm of
> the winter; but that is only an eye-blink, and the least
> space; and he soon comes from winter to winter again.
> So this life of men appears for a short space: what goes
> before it, or what follows after it, we know not. There-
> fore if this new lore brings aught more certain and
> more suitable, it is worthy of this, that we follow it."[39]

One of the most important results of Alfred's translation of Boethius was its contribution to his own intellectual development as well as to that of
Englishmen in his time and for generations to come.

Geoffrey Chaucer, probably one of the two or three
greatest writers in English history and possessor of
one of the most richly stored minds in fourteenth century England, could claim no greater learning in philosophy than the ninth century king had obtained and
then made available to others through his translation
of *De Consolatione*. F. N. Robinson, one of the twentieth century's foremost authorities on Chaucer, has
written that "most of the sustained passages of philosophical reflection in his poetry can be traced to Boethius." Robinson cites "the very heavy indebtedness of
the *Troilus*" and points to "strong Boethian influence"
in the Knight's Tale.[40] It was through *Boethius* that
many generations after Alfred learned most of the little that they knew of contributions to thought by Aristotle, and especially by Plato and Seneca.

Alfred succeeded marvelously in his Anglo-Saxon
rendering of *De Consolatione*. He not only translated a
Latin classic; he created an English one. The literary
superiority of Alfred's translation to Chaucer's, already alluded to, is not just a notion of biographers of
Alfred and scholars in Anglo-Saxon literature. So re-
doubtable a champion of Chaucerian eloquence as Robinson not only admits that Chaucer's Boethius is
inferior to Alfred's but even goes so far as to say of
the fourteenth century giant: "Indeed his prose at its
best (as in the freely composed introduction to the *As-
trolabe*)...is hardly equal to that of King Alfred's Anglo-Saxon Boethius."[41]

To let the reader make a comparison for himself,
one cannot do better than Oxford's Frederick Harrison in his celebrated Harvard lecture of 1901 on "The
Writings of King Alfred."[42] Professor Harrison quoted
first Alfred's, then Chaucer's, prose rendering of Boethius' hymn *O stelliferi conditor orbis*.

We reproduce here, as Harrison did, the translitera-
tion into modern English by W. J. Sedgefield, a rendering as remarkable for its fidelity to the rhythmic
roll of Alfred's prose as for its faithfulness to the actual words:

124

O thou Creator of heaven and earth, that ruleth on the eternal throne, Thou that maketh the heavens to turn in swift course and the stars to obey Thee, and the sun with his shining beams to quench the darkness of black night:...Thou that giveth short hours to the days of winter, and longer ones to those of summer, Thou that in harvest-tide with the strong north-east wind spoilest the trees of their leaves, and again in lententide givest them fresh ones with the soft south-west winds, lo! all creatures do Thy will, and keep the ordinances of Thy commandments, save man only; he setteth Thee at naught.[43]

The passage deserves the high praise that it has won from distinguished critics. As Harrison says, it has "rhythm, force, dignity, and purity of phrase."[44] This selection, as much as any in Alfred's Boethius, illustrates Stewart's[45] apt comment that the king's "prose is informed with intensity and fire, and possesses all the vigor and swing of verse" and Professor John Earle's statement that it has "a very genuine elevation without strain or effort."[46]

Note how far short of these qualities falls Chaucer's rendering of the same passage:

O thou maker of the wheel that beareth the stars, which that art fastened to thy perdurable chair, and turneth the heaven with ravishing sway, and constrainest the stars to suffer thy law; so that the moon sometime shining with her full horns, meeting with all the beams of the sun, her brother, hideth the stars that be less; and sometime, when the moon, pale with her dark horns, approacheth the sun, loseth her lights:...Thou restraineth the day by shorter dwelling, in the time of cold winter that maketh the leaves to fall. Thou dividest the swift tides of the night, when the hot summer is come. Thy might attempereth the variant seasons of the year; so that Zephyrus, the debonair wind, bringeth again in the first summer season the leaves that the wind hight Boreas hath reft away in autumn, that is to say, in the last end of summer. There is nothing unbound from his old law, nor forsakes the work of his proper estate. O thou governour governing all things by certain end, why refusest thou only to govern the works of men by due manner?[47]

A page by page comparison of the prose translations by Alfred and Chaucer confirms the superiority
of the king's work. Lest we lose perspective, however,
even Alfred's most devoted admirers must concede
that Chaucer's margin of superiority in verse far ex-
ceeds Alfred's in prose. Verse translations sometimes
attributed to the king, including portions of Boethius,[48] are mediocre.

When Alfred translated *De Consolatione* his mastery
of Latin was greater than when he rendered Orosius
into Anglo-Saxon. For example, as Germany's Dr. Hugo Schilling[49] and England's Charles Plummer[50] have
pointed out, between the times of the two translations
Alfred had gained an understanding of the triple
names of Roman nomenclature. Greater mastery of
mechanics gave him greater confidence, so that the
imagery in many places is more Alfredian than Boethian.

Alfred has sometimes been considered responsible
for the distinctly Christian character of some passages
of his translation of a work of pagan philosophy. But,
while Alfred evidently was in full agreement with the
Christian attitudes woven into the translation, he was
by no means their originator.[51] The medieval glosses
of the work, which he must have known either directly or through the clerical scholars at his court, had
grafted Christian interpretations onto a nonsectarian
declaration of faith in a Supreme Being that was the
quintessence of order and hence of ultimate justice in
the universe.[52]

But there is much to discuss that is Alfred's own.
The king's introduction, giving the story of Boethius'
life insofar as he knew it from the fragmentary and
partly legendary materials available to him, is a mas-
terpiece, as Harrison says, of "simple, pure, and
rhythmical English, as formed and lucid as the English of Bunyan or of Defoe."[53] He might have added
"or as the narratives of the King James Version of the
Bible."

And there are fresh metaphors with which Alfred,
in the body of the work, enlivens the dialogue be-

tween Philosophy and her imprisoned disciple, as
when he has Philosophy say:

> "When I rise aloft with these my servants we look
> down upon the storms of this world, even as the eagle
> does when he soars in stormy weather above the clouds
> where no winds can harm him."

Alfred speaks out, too, in the passage quoted in an
earlier chapter of this book, when he writes of the
"tools" that a king needs to do his job properly. And
again, when he says:

> Power is never a good thing, save its possessor be
> good, for, when power is beneficent, this is due to the
> man who wields it. You need not take thought for
> power nor endeavor after it, for if you are only wise
> and good, it will follow you, even though you seek it
> not.

His contempt is as vivid as his imagery in his picture of wicked rulers:

> We see them seated on high seats, bright with many
> kinds of raiment, decked with belts and golden-hilted
> swords and war dress of many kinds....But if you
> were to strip off his robes from such a one, and take
> away his company of retainers, then you would see that
> he is no more than any one of the thanes who serve
> him, if he be not someone of even lower degree.[54]

Alfred had learned at Athelney how little the trappings of kingship had to do with real kingliness.

And, in the same vein, the Golden Dragon of the
House of Wessex, scion of the proud line of Cerdic
the Saxon, writes:

> Lo! all men had the like beginning, coming from
> one father and one mother, and they are still brought
> forth alike. Why then do ye men pride yourselves
> above others without cause for your high birth, seeing
> ye can find no man but is high-born, and all men are
> of like birth, if ye will but bethink you of their begin-
> ning and their Creator? True high birth is of the mind,
> not of the flesh; and every man that is given over to
> vices forsaketh his Creator, and his origin, and his
> birth, and loseth rank till he fall to low estate.[55]

There is the much-praised prose hymn to the Omnipotent Spirit with which Alfred's Boethius closes, which has brought from Harrison the declaration, "I can find nothing more nobly expressed in the thousand years of English literature."[56]

> To God all is present, both that which was before and that which is now, yea, and that which shall be after us; all is present to Him. His abundance never waxeth, nor doth it ever wane. He never calleth aught to mind, for He hath forgotten naught. He looketh for naught, pondereth naught, for He knoweth all. He seeketh nothing, for He has lost nothing. He pursueth no creature, for none may flee from him; nor doth He dread aught, for none is more mighty than He, none is like unto Him. He is ever giving, yet He never waneth in aught. He is ever Almighty, for He ever willeth good and never evil.
>
> He needeth nothing. He is ever watching, never sleeping. He is ever equally beneficent. He is ever eternal, for the time never was when He was not, nor ever shall be. . . . Pray for what is right and needful for you, for He will not deny you. Hate evil, and flee from it. Love virtue and follow it. Whatsoever ye do is ever done before the Eternal and Almighty God; He seeth it all, and all He judges and will requite.[57]

Alfred's elaborate metaphor of God as axle-tree, though distasteful to R. H. Hodgkin, is much admired by others. P. J. Helm calls it "very powerful." F. Anne Payne sees it as a brilliant exposition of Alfred's theories of the workings of Wyrd, as distinguished from predestination. In any event, in its logical elaboration, it is somewhat reminiscent of John Donne and the metaphysical poets:

> . . . on the axle tree of a waggon the wheel turns, and the axle-tree stands still, and yet supports the whole waggon and regulates its progress. The wheel turns round, and the hub at the center moves more firmly and securely than the rim does. Now the axle is as it were the Highest Good, which we call God, and the best men move nearest to God just as the hub moves nearest to the axle. . . . But the rims of wheels depend on the spoke, though they all wallow on the earth; so

the worst men depend on the average, and the average on the best, and the best on God. Even though the worst turn all their love to this world, they are not able to remain there, or to become anything, if they are not in any part fastened to God, any more than the felloes [parts of the rim] of the wheel can make any progress if they are not fastened to the spokes, and the spokes to the axle-tree. The parts of the rim are farthest from the axle-tree; therefore they go the most roughly. The hub goes nearest to the axle; therefore it goes the most securely. So do the best men. As they place their love nearer to God, and more despise these earthly things, so are they more free from care, and are less anxious how fortune may vary, or what it may bring.[58]

Alfred pursues the simile in greater detail in subsequent lines. As one commentator has said: "From this point of view the wheel is seen to embrace society as a whole, as well as the single individual, and though men may freely choose to place themselves near God at the hub or to wallow with the rim in the filth of the earth, they, whatever their decisions, are nevertheless bound to other men and to God."[59]

Alfred's imagery of the wheel is much more elaborate than in the commentary of Remigius, which seems to have been the gloss upon which he chiefly or solely relied.[60]

The magnitude and subtlety of Alfred's achievement in recreating the Boethius in a way expressive of his personal beliefs and meaningful to his people became apparent only in 1968 with publication of F. Anne Payne's masterly work *King Alfred and Boethius: An Analysis of the Old English Version of the Consolation of Philosophy*. Miss Payne convincingly demonstrated that the king's departures from the Latin text were in no wise the result of an inability to translate the sections excised or a failure to comprehend the philosophical refinements of "the last of the Romans." They were, on the contrary, essential to the consistency and coherence of Alfred's fusion of Greek and Christian philosophy with the Anglo-Saxon concept of Wyrd to expound a sophisticated resolution of the problems of free will and predestination. Alfred sees order and natural law as predestined (forethought) while "Wyrd controls the immediate, daily, contingent permutations and combinations that are possible to all things within the boundaries of what is ordained."[61] Alfred sees both man and the Animating Essence of the universe as "free of the necessity of fatal order."[62] Astonishingly enough, as Miss Payne points out, "Alfred's solution to this ancient problem has more similarities to those of the recent writers William James and Paul Tillich than to those of Boethius and St. Augustine."[63]

Beatrice Lees has said of the Anglo-Saxon Boethius, "Here, if anywhere, the dead Alfred yet speaks with a living voice, telling of his hopes and fears, his ambitions and difficulties, his ideals and disappointments."[64] For many of us, that voice seems to speak more directly than in the celebrated rhetoric, in such simple statements as the often quoted: "I have longed to live worthily all my life, and thus to leave to those who shall come after me my memory in good works." Was this not the reputation that Beowulf achieved, he whose people "bemoaned the fate of their mighty lord; said he was kindest of earthly kings, mildest, most gentle, most eager for fame"?

Alfred, in his forties, a much more advanced stage of life in the ninth century than in the twentieth, was mindful of mortality. It is not strange that he should be. He had already lived longer than each of his brothers, and since his twentieth year he had not lived a day without pain or the threat of it.

While Alfred doubtless had found consolation in philosophy, he had not yet found tranquility. He tells us so in the preface to his next work, a translation of *Saint Augustine's Soliloquies.* He tells how he surveyed the forest of philosophy, practicing a rigid selectivity, so that he brought home with him only those timbers useful to him in the construction of a fit habitation for his mind. "In each tree I saw something that I needed at home. Therefore I exhort all who are able, and have the wagons [to bear the load] to direct their steps to the self-same forest where I cut the stud-shafts. Let them there obtain more for themselves, and load their wagons with fir branches, so that they may weave many a neat wall, and erect many a rare house, and build a fair enclosure, and therein dwell in joy and comfort both winter and summer, in such manner as I have not yet done."[65]

He then draws a parallel between the house of philosophy, or "temporary cottage," and the final dwelling of the soul, or "home everlasting," and expresses the hope: "May He who created both and ruleth both, grant me to be fit for each—both here to be useful and thither to attain."[66]

Then Alfred introduces his translation of Augustine's work in simple words ideally suited to readers not versed in philosophical terminology:

"Augustine, bishop of Carthage, made two books about his own mind. These books are called soliloquies, that is, concerning the meditations and doubts of his mind—how his reason answered his mind when the mind doubted about anything, or wished to know anything that it could not before clearly understand."

The selection of the *Soliloquies* for his next translation was a natural one. They enjoyed considerable prestige; they were written by the same Augustine, bishop of Hippo, who instructed Orosius; and they were, like the Boethius, the creations of a neo-Platonist.

Alfred's revisions and interpolations are so numerous that the first soliloquy is, by actual word count, more Alfred's than Augustine's, and the second soliloquy, which the king calls "the anthology of the second book," and the third book are almost entirely Alfred's work. The king longs to know not only whether his spirit is indestructible, but also "whether I, after the parting of the body and the soul, shall ever know more than I now know of all that which I have long wished to know; for I cannot find anything better in man than that he know, and anything worse than that he be ignorant."[67]

He asks, "What would I care for life if I knew nothing?"[68]

Alfred concludes that the highest wisdom is "the
highest good," and to him this is the path to God.
And he says of every man, "So much as he loves wisdom, so much does he love God."[69] To seek truth is to
search for God. But men come to wisdom by different
paths. "Therefore methinks that man very foolish and
very wretched who will not increase his intelligence
while he is in this world, and also wish and desire that
he may come to the eternal life, where nothing is hid
from us."[70] The pursuit of knowledge is for Alfred
not merely a duty, but a passion. He who would know
wisdom "must press his bare body to it."

*　　*　　*

Alfred's literary labors, from the first, had been inspired by his passion to acquire and share knowledge.
In fulfilling that desire, he had given his people a reasonably complete prose literature in their own language. He had given them a history of the world, a
geography of Europe and parts of Asia and Africa, a
history of their own island, a manual for guidance in
posts of ecclesiastical or civil responsibility, a story
book, a summary of much of the philosophy of ancient Greece and Rome, an attractive presentation of
Christian philosophy, and a number of vividly expressed observations based on his scholarship and his
practical experience as a resourceful and imaginative
statesman.

Many persons have wondered why Alfred, a genius
and a man of such celebrated integrity as to be known
in history as "the Truthteller," should so freely have
added to the works that he translated without signify-
ing that the interpolations were his own and not the
original authors'. Is it not probable that in so doing
Alfred reflected the culture of which he was a prod-
uct? He dearly loved from childhood the verse narratives chanted by the scops, each embellishing the story
he told with anything that he thought would delight
or instruct. Each man must tell the tale as well as he
could, but no one would be so immodest as to inter-

rupt the narration to claim credit for the inventions
with which he adorned what had been transmitted to
him.

In making his versions of Latin classics available to
his countrymen in their own language, Alfred probably accomplished more than he knew. He was not
only the first composer of enduring English literary
prose. As Kemp Malone has pointed out: "Most important of all, he gave prestige to prose composition
in English, and thereby opened the way to the cultiva-
tion of important literary genres hitherto neglected."[71]
The late tenth and eleventh centuries would become
known as the classic age of Anglo-Saxon prose. To the
fields into which Alfred had ventured would be added
that of scientific writing.[72] The development of the
English language was almost incalculably accelerated
by the king's efforts. As Sir Frank Stenton has
stressed, "for the expression of thought and of more
than the barest elements of learning, English prose
was still an untried instrument when he began to
write. The management of an elaborate sentence was
an experimental business. . . ."[73] But Alfred succeeded
so well that, as Sir James Murray declared, "In literary
culture the Normans were about as far behind the
people whom they conquered as the Romans were
when they made themselves masters of Greece." Alfred produced works which survived the Norman
conquest, which indeed were copied afresh in Norman England.[74] Except for Alfred's work in creating
for his people both a viable literary prose and a valuable prose literature, and in unifying the people for
whom these creations were intended, English culture
would have been eradicated by the efficient and energetic Normans. Instead, the vigorous culture of the
English survived its inferior Norman rival. The testimony of John Richard Greene, John Earl, Stopford
Brooke, R. W. Chambers, and a host of others to
Alfred's role as the "father of English prose," when
viewed in the context of his defense by education, military science, and diplomacy of the culture to whose
development he so richly contributed, reveals Alfred

as a man of accomplishment unparalleled in medieval or modern history. We have the language of Churchill, and Mark Twain, and Dickens, and Shakespeare, and Chaucer because it was first of all the language of Alfred. And, because of his vision, his daring, and his dedication, it is today, in all its unrivaled variety, the language of dwellers in lands unknown to that pioneer geographer, and the vehicle of more of the world's transactions than ever was the case with the Latin whose decline he lamented.

XI

SOLON OF THE SAXONS

a man should be able to fight, without incurring a blood feud, if he found his wife under the same blanket with another man. No one should doubt that. But suppose a husband should find his spouse behind locked doors with the offender. Could he then attack with equal impunity?

And what if a man should be assaulted by one who left a two-inch wound in his forehead? Should the fine be the same for a wound above the hairline, where there was a probability of hirsute concealment, as for one so low as to leave a permanently visible scar?

If a man should take hold of a nun's breast without her permission, was the offense more or less heinous than if she were someone's wife?

Should a virgin be more richly compensated for rape than an unmarried woman of experience?

If a man's thumbnail was struck off by another, was he entitled to more compensation than if the nail of the third finger had been torn away?

All of the foregoing questions were dealt with by the mind that translated Orosius, produced a classic in

European geography, and wrestled with the problems
of predestination versus free will as set forth in the
pages of *Boethius*. Despite the fact that the art, the architecture, and the literature of the Anglo-Saxons evidence the vitality of their civilization, one who studies
their laws is likely to conclude that Alfred, as the supreme judge in his kingdom, was obliged to "mete
and dole unequal laws unto a savage race." As a matter of fact, sophistication in the law is not an inevitable accompaniment of the flowering of civilization.
Homer's Greece was more richly creative than Hadri-
an's Rome but in matters of law Homeric Greece, red-
der with blood feuds than with its celebrated rosy
fingered dawns, was much nearer to ninth century
England than to the chaste white facade of Hadrianic
justice. Whether Alfred was capable of preparing a
scientifically categorized code of law for his people is
an academic consideration; most assuredly, like all the
other peoples of Northern Europe, they were not prepared to receive such a code. Alfred did provide a
code that brought a large measure of uniformity to
the administration of justice in England, reforming
without destroying, bringing a softened expression of
humanity to the ancient lineaments of the law.

Of course, even Alfred's justice may seem to us
cold-eyed and cleaver faced. He possessed no wizard-
ry to transform law instantly and yet leave her recog-
nizable. The practical reformer, particularly in
matters of humanitarianism and the law, must frequently do less well than he knows. Thus Jefferson's
reforms of the Code of Virginia, though significant,
are ballasted with practical considerations that prevent
their ascension to the level of his idealism. And
George Mason the constitution-maker perforce compromises the ideals of George Mason author of the
Bill of Rights.

Alfred's success in legal reform, though considerable, was limited by the power of official precedent,
the sacredness of popular custom, the primacy of the
clan concept, and the primitive nature of the judicial
machinery available. It is easy to say that Alfred could

have created new machinery, but an examination of the problem may make the suggestion seem glib.

The Anglo-Saxons knew nothing of that conquering majesty of the law celebrated by some Mediterranean peoples. If Justice was enthroned among them, she sat by sufferance, prepared to yield her seat at a moment's notice to the superior demands of blood. It was Alfred's self-imposed task to elevate the claims of the community above the clan concept of honor.

The machinery available to him was rudimentary in form but complex in the nuances of its operation. There were folk moots, or local courts, in many parts of England. These were often the courts of original jurisdiction. No sable curtain or paneled wall was the backdrop of justice in these assemblies. The drama of litigation was played out in an open field with the chalk downs as ancient witnesses or a forest of oaks as silent spectators. Sometimes the ocean's roar was a mighty counterpoint to the sing-song recital of a plaintiff. No bewigged judges heard the case. A man's cause was judged by his peers, like as not tan-faced freemen more accustomed to working in the sunlight than in the glow of a study lamp. Sometimes the court of original jurisdiction was the great hall of an earl, bishop or other local magnate who presided over causes originating in his area of domination. In such instances, the judge sometimes was the protector of one of his own accused thanes. Often, as we know from Alfred's efforts to educate these provincial jurists, they committed injustices more from ignorance than from malevolence. There were many opportunities for justice to miscarry at the local level through the ignorance and passions of the folk moot or the ignorance and partisanship of the magnate's court.

Fortunately cases could be appealed from a lower court to the king who, in the way of his fathers, heard complaints from his people in his progress about the nation. The sovereign was the original circuit rider. The ruler was aided by his Witan and, of course, brought to the administration of justice the majesty of his person and the force of that "divinity that doth

hedge about a king." Even so, the proceedings were
far more informal than any that we are likely to asso-
ciate with a high court in any English-speaking nation
today. An Anglo-Saxon illuminated manuscript of
Genesis (Claudius MS. B. IV) depicts Pharaoh presid-
ing at the trial of his chief baker. Just as the anach-
ronisms of Italian Renaissance renderings of Biblical
scenes afford clues to the dress and customs of fourteenth century Italy, so this representation of Pharoah
as judge tells us something of Anglo-Saxon trials with
the king sitting in judgment. The king wears a crown
and holds a scepter in one hand and a sword in the
other. Since the trial depicted is for a capital offense,
the use of the sword—even if followed by Alfred—
may have been restricted to the pronouncement of
the death sentence. Apart from the crown, the king's
dress is such as he might wear on most other occasions. There are no judicial robes, only the usual
cloak pinned with a shoulder clasp, and the long tunic
from which peep pointed-toed shoes. On either side
of him sit members of the Witan, similarly garbed except for their conical hats. There is no reason to think
there was any additional royal panoply at sessions of
Alfred's court except for the emblem of the Golden
Dragon, reminder of the ancient and supposedly divine origins of the House of Wessex. In many cases
that today would be denominated chancery, as distinguished from criminal, causes, the appearance of the
court was decidedly more informal than the illuminated manuscript would suggest. We have the sworn testimony of one man that, when he sought a ruling in a
property suit, he was ushered into the private chambers of one of the king's country houses. Alfred, interrupted in washing his hands, returned to his
ablutions, then paused to hear the details and rendered judgment on the spot.[1] The man apparently related the occurrence not so much as one recounting
an unusual experience but rather as one providing
circumstantial detail as evidence of the reliability of
his memory. We do not see in Alfred any signs of an
insouciance akin to that of the nineteenth century En-

glish chancellor who heard a case while swimming, with opposing attorneys making their pleas from opposite banks of the stream. Rather, we see a monarch who held few private moments sacred from public duty.

Like the lesser tribunals of its day, the king's court functioned without lawyers. The idea of the law as a separate profession would be foreign to Englishmen until the twelfth century. A typical trial was a contest of oaths umpired by the sovereign. A man's case was deemed proved if he could obtain a sufficient number of men in good standing to swear to the truth of it.[2] The number of oaths necessary depended upon the nature of the crime and the rank of those subscribing to the oath. The value of a man's oath was proportionate to his status and was easily determined with precision since each man had his wergild. A preponderant weight of oaths on one side of a case might send the opposing side scurrying about to add oaths to its weight of testimony. If the accused did not have enough "oath-helpers" to free him, he had to submit to trial by ordeal. Among the Anglo-Saxons this was usually a matter of the accused plunging his hand into boiling water. If the hand healed with ease, he was regarded as innocent.[3] Primitive indeed, but so entrenched was trial by ordeal that it persisted in England until Innocent III's Fourth Lateran Council deprived it of all religious sanction in 1215. In fact, even King Henry III's decree of abolition four years later did not end the practice in some remote parts of the kingdom.[4] The custom antedated the people's experience with Christianity and was based on the assumption that supernatural influences would intervene to determine innocence or guilt. Of course, many physical factors help to determine the extent of injury under exposure to burning, but psychological factors may play a part too. Modern science confirms that a subject hypnotized into believing that red hot coals are being placed on his forearm will sometimes blister on the spots to which ice cubes are applied. Psychosomatic factors may sometimes have increased the severity of burns acquired by ordeal and inhibited their healing. Trial by ordeal was illogical and unjust but perhaps no more so than some of the supposedly more sophisticated methods of determination that succeeded it.

Trial by ordeal, in one form or another, is deeply engrained in human experience, reaching from barbarism into civilization and extending over the continents of Europe, Asia, Africa, and North and South America. Strangely enough, one quite general form of decision by ordeal—trial by combat—was not practiced by ninth century Englishmen though it was embodied in the laws of nearly all the German tribes from which they sprang. This custom was later introduced into England, being specifically exempted by Henry III in the proclamation in which he abolished all other forms of ordeal. In a resort to the arbitrament of arms, the victor was declared innocent as a result of divine intervention. This custom survived for centuries in the office of king's champion, a knight who represented in combat the validity of his sovereign's claims. Trial by combat in England was not abolished by statute until 1819. Some may say that it survives in a troubled twentieth century in which nations have repeatedly resorted to war, proclaiming that the righteousness of their cause will be proved when God crowns it with victory.

Determining the extent of a man's guilt was not always a simple matter of trial by ordeal after establishing that an offense had been committed. Anglo-Saxon law recognized certain obligations that circumscribed the freedom with which the individual might act, certain loyalties which could mitigate the seriousness of his transgression. Foremost of these, as we have suggested, was the bond of blood. A man was expected to be the avenger of his kinsman and kinswoman. Of course, there was the concomitant responsibility to make amends for the misdeeds of kindred. Unlike some clan or tribal societies placing strong emphasis on the obligations of consanguinity, the Anglo-Saxon culture construed such responsibilities as applying to relationship in the maternal as well as the paternal lines.[5]

Another obligation circumscribing a man's independence of action was the loyalty that he owed his lord. This could be the responsibility of slave to master or of a thane in the comitatus of an earl. The king was already recognized as overlord. Here was inchoate the feudalism of a later age.

Once the convicted man's offense was weighed in the balance with any mitigating circumstances, his punishment was determined. In general, when Alfred came to the throne, *lex talionis* prevailed. Quite literally the price of violence was an eye for an eye and a tooth for a tooth. Fines were also exacted. Many people of our day will find it strange that the Anglo-Saxons had no jails. Confinement was seldom used as a punishment. The accused was seldom bound or shackled except to insure his appearance for trial, and trials were not long delayed. Usually a man was simply bound over on his honor to appear for trial. Ordinarily this was sufficient guarantee. If one charged with a serious offense should run away he would be officially outlawed, i.e., anyone in any part of the kingdom could kill him with impunity. Between his concern for his reputation and his fears for his life, a man usually proved compliant.[6]

Of course, the courts not only dealt with criminal matters but also rendered decisions in what we today would call chancery suits. The record of equity in the Anglo-Saxon courts is a very difficult one to bring into focus. Partly because people seldom trouble to reduce to writing definitions that have long been commonly accepted, we are not even sure of the nuances of meaning of the labels—folk land and book land—applied to the two principal divisions of property in Alfred's England. Some things we do know. *Boc* or *booc*, besides meaning *book* in the present day sense, also meant charter.[7] The Old English charters (books) are mostly grants of land made by the king to nobles, bishops, or religious houses. By the ninth century, the charter usually stated that the grant was made with

the consent of the Witan. Sir Frederick Pollock and
Frederick William Maitland, with other distinguished
scholars of the law, have held that such a royal grant
probably did not mean the displacement of those already dwelling on the land in question. The book
land charter, they believe, was simply a "grant of lord-
ship and revenues."[8] In this respect, a royal grant of
book land was not only analogous to the *Alodium* of
England's Norman kings, but also analogous to those
of proprietaries in America which still later English
kings granted to their favorites in the seventeenth
century. Since one receiving book land from his sovereign sometimes granted portions to his own dependents, thus creating subgrants of the same character,
controversies over book land could lead to complex
litigation. Although the judicial functions of the king's
court were ordinarily strictly appelate, suits involving
book land were often carried directly to the king and
his Witan. After all, the original grant had been made
by the king with the Witan's consent.

The term *folk land* is even more shadowy than *book
land*. The most reliable scholarship seems to indicate
that folk land was land held by custom, or habit, rather than by written law. Thus all land not disposed of
by charter was folk land.[9] The problems of disposing
of land held by long occupancy but without written title must have presented many legal difficulties. Suits
involving folk land, however, would be tried initially
in the folk moot, though of course the decision of that
body might be appealed to the king.

From time to time Anglo-Saxon kings reduced elements of the law to writing. They did not see themselves as law makers; as Cam has said, "Almost
certainly law was older than kingship."[10] Nor were
they codifiers of law; their efforts were not systematic
enough to be described as codification. They sought
to preserve the law and to make its provisions available for reference; they therefore became its record-
ers. Near the beginning of the seventh century King
Ethelbert I of Kent created the earliest English document when he issued a set of laws for his people.[1]

Perhaps Augustine convinced him of the desirability of written laws; the Roman monk's mission to Britain at Gregory's behest was undertaken in Ethelbert's reign. Augustine was familiar with the written laws of the Romans. The influence of Augustine seems evident in the introduction to Ethelbert's laws ("These are the decrees which King Ethelbert established in the lifetime of Augustine") and in their first provision ("[Theft of] God's property and the Church's shall be compensated twelvefold..."). As the years passed no man made bold to assume the role of one who had stretched the fabric of the law to cover more problems. The decrees of Ilothhere and Eadric, Ethelbert's successors on the throne of Kent, declared that they "extended the laws which their predecessors had made...."[12] One of their successors, Wihtred, prefaced another issuance of laws with an account of a deliberative assembly of church and lay magnates convened by the king: "There the notables, with the consent of all, drew these decrees, and added them to the legal usages of the people of Kent...."[13]

A contemporary of Wihtred's, King Ine of Wessex, drew up the first written law of the West Saxons. Interestingly enough, the twenty-eighth provision of Wihtred's laws is almost identical in wording with the twentieth provision in Ine's. "If a man from afar, or a stranger, travels through a wood off the highway and neither shouts nor blows a horn, he shall be assumed to be a thief, and as such may be either slain or put to ransom." This near identity in the two sets of laws has puzzled many scholars. Since this provision in each kingdom's laws dealt with the conduct prescribed for a stranger "from afar" traveling within its borders and with the treatment that might be accorded him if his actions aroused suspicion, is it not possible that the two rulers, each mindful of disputes that might arise over the fate of his subjects when traveling in the other's realms, sought by uniformity to obviate these difficulties?

The next compilation of laws in Wessex, some two centuries later, was the work of Ine's collateral descen-

143

dant, Alfred the Great. The exact date is unknown. Liebermann, probably the most thorough scholar of Anglo-Saxon law, suggests 892-893,[14] while Attenborough favors the possibility of an earlier year. In any event, Alfred had made for himself an opportunity not enjoyed by any of his predecessors; he had it within his power to promulgate laws for the entire English nation.[15] Alfred's pronouncement of his laws, therefore, was an event unique in English history. He was historian enough to appreciate its uniqueness, and statesman enough to disguise its singularity. He brought forth the infant body of laws swaddled in the vestments of antiquity.

Of the seventy-seven chapters comprising the laws of Alfred, the first forty-eight were devoted to an introduction including an Old English translation of the Ten Commandments, quotations from the Book of Exodus and the Acts of the Apostles, and an account of the growth of ecclesiastical law through both ecumenical and English councils. Reliance on the Bible as a basis for English law would continue for centuries. In 1607, the year that saw the successful transfer of English law to the New World, a Jamestown jury indicted Captain John Smith "upon a Chapter in Leviticus."[16] Threads of Roman law destined to endure as part of the English legal fabric first entered it as ravelings from tangled skeins of ecumenical controversy. Alfred skillfully invoked ancient sanction without sacrifice of flexibility, concluding the introduction with the statement that compensations for the misdeeds of men had been ordained and recorded at many councils with varying provisions. Incidentally, this comment also exemplified the prevalently negative aspect of the law in Old England, as in most of the ancient and medieval world.

Following this general introduction setting forth biblical and church sources, Alfred in two paragraphs links his laws specifically to the Mercian and West Saxon heritages of his subjects. At the same time, he successfully invokes a sense of history to make his own decrees seem a natural link between those of his

144

predecessors and those that his successors might find necessary to promulgate.

"Now I, King Alfred, have collected these laws and have given orders for copies to be made of many of those which our predecessors observed and which I myself approved of. But many of those I did not approve of I have annulled, by the advice of my councillors, while [in other cases] I have ordered changes to be introduced."[17]

A nice balance, this, that the king has struck between respect for tradition and for the opinions of his councillors on the one hand, and positive assertion of his own royal authority on the other. He follows with an apparently modest statement of his desire not to infringe upon his successors' rights to promulgate laws as they see fit and thus by implication asserts his own right to amend the pronouncements of his predecessors: "For I have not dared to presume to set down in writing many [changes] of my own, for I cannot tell what [innovations of mine] will meet with the approval of our successors."

And then he reminds his people of his laws' spiritual descent from those of three revered precursors while simultaneously recalling for the benefit of his blood-conscious folk the fact of his actual physical descent from one of them:

> But those which were the most just of the laws I found—whether they dated from the time of Ine my kinsman, or of Offa, king of the Mercians, or of Ethelbert, who was the first [king] to be baptized in England—these I have collected while rejecting the others.

The next sentence strikes again the nice balance between derived authority and personal assertion, this time to achieve a note of inevitability.

> I, then, Alfred, king of the West Saxons, have shown these to all my councillors, and they have declared that it met with the approval of all, that they should be observed.

Ine had begun the enumeration of his laws with the assertion, "In the first place, we command that the

145

servants of God heed, and duly observe, their proper rule."

"In the first place we command...." In almost the same words Alfred began the listing of his laws. But the conclusion of his sentence was different: "In the first place we enjoin you, as a matter of supreme importance, that every man shall abide carefully by his oath and his pledge." Thus Alfred at the outset reminded his people that fidelity was the keystone to the vault of justice he was erecting over their heads. Without a sincere effort to keep oaths and pledges, the structure was more a threat than a protection. The king had found a focal point for his laws.

But Alfred was not one to magnify a virtue until, by exaggeration, it became a vice. Not all oaths were sacred. "If anyone is wrongfully constrained to promise either of these: to betray his lord or to render aid in an unlawful undertaking, then it is better to be false [to the promise] than to perform it." The substance of virtue mattered more to Alfred than any abstraction.

"If, however, he pledges himself to something which it is lawful to carry out and proves false to his pledge, he shall humbly give his weapons and possessions to his friends to keep and remain forty days in prison at a royal manor, and undergo there whatever the bishop prescribes for him...."

The imprisonment here referred to seems to have been a sort of house arrest rather than a jailing in the modern sense. Nevertheless, the punishment was sufficient to emphasize the seriousness of the offense.

The gravity of a crime was determined in part by its nature and in part by the circumstances of its commission. The king's courts and the churches were the two great symbols and enforcers of law and order; a crime committed in the king's presence or within an ecclesiastical edifice acquired a deeper dye of infamy. Four crimes, wherever committed, were capital offenses: treachery to one's lord, arson, burglary, and murder. The number of capital offenses under the laws inherited by Alfred was far smaller than in some later centuries, as, for instance, in the "spacious days of

Elizabeth" when a little girl might be hanged for the theft of a pocket handkerchief or a hungry small boy for the stealing of a loaf of bread. Nor in Saxon times had England devised those exquisite tortures which would prove its sophistication in later generations, as in the days of King James I when the public amputation of the convicted man's genitals might precede the cutting off of his head and the quartering of his body.

But even the comparatively limited use of capital punishment in his time was too much for Alfred's taste. He was humane by nature and shared the view of the English church that man should not lightly destroy God's handiwork. Wherever possible he tried to substitute fines for physical punishment. Alfred provided specific payments for particular offenses. Not content to state principles of justice, he specified the details of its administration. He gave detailed answers to the problems of justice posed in the first paragraphs of this chapter. The man who found his wife behind closed doors with another man had a right to fight the usurper without incurring a blood feud. Should the penalty for a wound below the hairline be greater than for one above? "If a wound an inch long is inflicted under the hair, one shilling shall be given as compensation. If a wound an inch long is inflicted in front of the hair, two shillings as compensation." Equally specific was the provision: "If anyone lustfully seizes a nun, either by her clothes or by her breast, without her permission, he shall pay as compensation twice the sum we have fixed in the case of a woman belonging to the laity." And so on: "If anyone rapes a girl who is not of age, the same compensation shall be paid to her as is paid to an adult." If anyone rapes the slave of a commoner, he shall pay five shillings to the commoner, and a fine of sixty shillings. If a slave rapes a slave, castration shall be required as compensation." There was even a precise answer to the question, "If a man's thumbnail is struck off by another, is he entitled to more compensation than if the nail of the third finger had been torn away?" Five shillings for the thumbnail, two for a nail of the third finger.

Primitive the code is in many ways, but even in its particularities it marks an advance over something more primitive. A clause declares, "Formerly to steal gold or horses or bees brought higher fines. Now all thefts, except the abducting of human beings, meet the same penalty." The hint of the earlier code reminds us of the value of horses in a primitive society, as in frontier days of the American West when horse stealing was a capital offense. Bees were doubtless particularly important to a people who, in some of their most seraphic strains of song, celebrated the virtues of mead.

More significant is Alfred's effort, already remarked, to substitute fines for physical punishment. Careful distinctions between homicide and murder made it possible to force the offender to compensate the family of the person killed rather than to pay with his own life. Perhaps even more important was Alfred's determined effort to substitute the remedy of the law for the vengeance of the blood feud. Let the victim of an injury "ride to the earl and ask for help. If he will not help him, let him ride to the king before he fights." Though the king was not so quixotic as to attempt to abolish slavery overnight, he did prescribe that slaves be given their freedom when their masters had violated their rights, not only by physical cruelty but even by requiring them to work on a legal holiday. Even more significant of a new dispensation was Alfred's stern admonition: "Judge not one judgment for the rich, and another for the poor." A realist as well as an idealist, the king would have agreed with Plato that perfect justice is unobtainable in the affairs of men. But at least, as ruler, he publicly and solemnly renounced the view of Thrasymachus, honored more often than breached, that "justice is the interest of the stronger." The Golden Dragon had become the Draco of his people.

Helping the king in the administration of justice was the Witan, which, as we have seen, approved his laws in the first instance. Some nineteenth century historians, eager for democratic precedents, thought of the Witan as a representative body and a few even suggested that it had originated in popular election. At least one distinguished historian of that period, however, W. Stubbs, advanced the view in which most scholars now concur, that the members of the Witan were merely royal retainers serving at the pleasure of the prince. In 1905 the careful scholarship of H. Munro Chadwick made the conclusion almost inescapable.[18]

Is it not possible, however, that the Witan was in a very narrow sense representative, not of the people but of the aristocracy? Representative, like the assemblage of lords temporal and spiritual at Runnymede in 1215, of the chief estates of the realm? The king doubtless appointed the members of the Witan but practical necessity must have all but dictated the naming of certain magnates, noble and ecclesiastical.

Yet the convening of the Witan appears always to have been at the king's pleasure and the members of Alfred's council appear never to have entertained the notion of dominating him. He asserted his mastery when he first called the Witan to hear his accounting for his guardianship of the royal inheritance and he never relinquished his supremacy. Though not originally zealous to be king, Alfred was never content to be sovereign in name only.

Each great earl, or ealdorman,[19] was the chief man of a shire, charged with the responsibility of leading the men of the country in battle and with coming to the aid of any injured person within his territory who sought legal restitution. It is certainly logical to assume that so wise a king as Alfred would consult with a figure of such importance when dealing with events in his shire. It is also reasonable to assume that in many matters he would seek the collective judgment of the bishops and ealdormen. Advice undoubtedly traveled up as well as down the conduits of justice.

Whatever the private dispositions of the magnates as they presided over justice in their own shires, they operated under the watchful eye of a king who had in his laws issued a stern admonition:

That which you will that other men should not do to you, that do you not to them. From this one Doom a man may understand how he should judge everyone justly; he needs no other doombook. Let him judge a man as he himself would wish to be judged, if the other man were in his place.

To Alfred these words were more than rhetoric. He habitually gave a patient ear and an assiduous mind to any man or woman who complained of injustice. And, in those times of royal progresses through the land, the king would eventually be accessible to the poorest subject who felt himself wronged. An audience with their sovereign, even when the ruler proved to be a nation-maker whose hours were filled with action and meditation, was easily obtained in those uncomplicated days even by the humble ones who in subsequent centuries would be kept waiting on aldermen's doorsteps.

XII

THE LAST FIGHT

*t*hough Alfred could bring law and order to his kingdom, the king's peace could still be breached by external enemies. In the late autumn of 892, he received a jolting reminder of this hard fact.

At that time Alfred's pleased contemplation of advances in learning and the arts and in the administration of justice—in short, in all the pursuits of peace made possible by fourteen years of freedom from fullscale warfare with the Danes—was interrupted by news that another Great Army of the Vikings was sailing to England from Boulogne.[1] Had this, men asked, been the portent of the "long-haired star" that had appeared a few months before and which the scholars of the church had dismissed as a *cometa*? The Straits of Dover were white-furrowed with the swift approach of about 250 dragon ships. These vessels entered the mouth of the Lympne River in East Kent and moved upstream four miles to the Weald, or wilderness country. There thousands of warriors disembarked with their horses and there, if Alfred's orders had been carried out, their progress would have been arrested by a strong fortification. But the king's efforts to defend England had been hampered again by the dilatoriness of the peasantry, against which, according to Asser, he often had cause to complain. The invaders found only a half-finished fort and easily subdued the laborers inside. It was convenient for the Danes to take over half-constructed defenses which could be converted for their own use.

The Great Army was barely settled in when the appearance off the Thames estuary of eighty boldstriped sails revealed the presence of a second Viking fleet. There could be no doubt that the two forces were acting in unison. The second army was led by Haesten, who more than thirty years before had terrorized the Mediterranean coasts of Spain, Provence, and Italy and a few years later had killed in a single skirmish two of the greatest Frankish leaders. One of these victims was Count Robert the Strong, father of Odo, now king of France. Odo had become king after Charles the Fat, last of the Carolingian rulers, was forced to surrender the interior of his kingdom to the Vikings. The Norsemen had penetrated still deeper into France before meeting resistance when they found themselves too far from the sea that was their element. Now they saw no reason to linger in a land that they had reduced to famine. The green fields and sleek herds of England tempted Haesten and other northmen to test Alfred's defenses again. The coordination of the two invading armies became obvious as they dug in on either side of the great wood, one hundred twenty miles or more long, that stretched a width of thirty miles between them. If they successfully closed the pincers, the eastern half of Kent would be theirs.

Equally disturbing was the probability of cooperation from the Danes of neighboring East Anglia. Even Guthrum, most trustworthy of the Danish chieftains, had once been unable to resist the temptation to cooperate with Viking invaders against his royal godfather. Now Guthrum had been dead about two years and Alfred could count on none of the remaining chieftains to restrain the Danes of East Anglia. United ac-

tion between the Danelaw and the invading armies could put the entire west coast of England under alien control. Alfred required from East Anglia a renewed oath that the peace would be kept and accepted six hostages as a guarantee. He also drew a fresh pledge from the Danes of Northumbria.

Calling out the fyrd, Alfred led it to a position equidistant between the two invading armies. But he did not abandon diplomacy. He welcomed Haesten as a friend and arranged for the baptism of his sons, with Alfred himself godfather to one and Ethelred of Mercia to the other. The king made a substantial gift of money and goods to Haesten and the Viking chieftain "bound himself with oaths." Soon afterward he moved his men and his fleet northward across the Thames to Benfleet, near the border with East Anglia.

Alfred undoubtedly was far from confident that he had purchased peace. He did hope that he had bought a little time.

Early in 893 that little ran out. Both invading armies plundered widely and, in the words of the *Chronicle*, "as often as the other Danish armies went out in full force,...those of the Danelaw went either with them or on their behalf."[2] Like Beowulf, Alfred, after years of peaceful rule, had to gird on his armor in his latter days to do battle with the dragon.

Saxon bands patrolled forest paths day and night in search of Danish marauders. Alfred's reform of the fyrd, permitting one half to remain at home for farm work while the other half performed military duties, made possible an unremitting hunt. And the burhs that he had established enabled soldiers to sally forth to intercept the enemy and quickly return to the security of fortification. Alfred's principal effort was to frustrate the plundering expeditions wherever possible and to prevent the enemy armies from uniting. Hodgkin has suggested that Alfred's strategy, Fabian in character, indicates that the king had profited in a very practical way from his recent reading of Orosius.[3]

The shift to more massive maneuvers and clashes was presaged when the fleet of the Great Army left base at Appledore on the Lympne to join Haesten's ships at Benfleet on the north bank of the Thames. The concentration of vessels gave them command of the water approaches to London, the most considerable town in England. In April the Great Army abandoned its policy of avoiding direct confrontation with the Anglo-Saxon forces and swept through Hampshire and Alfred's native Berkshire before turning east in an effort to join Haesten's army at Benfleet. At Farnham they were suddenly confronted by an English army under Prince Edward, Alfred's eldest son. The king thrilled as sovereign and as father to the news that the young man had beaten the enemy and was driving them before him. As Alfred hurried from the west to join his son, he rejoiced that the trap was working so well. Then came news that the Danelaw had erupted. At that very moment an army from Northumbria and East Anglia was attacking Exeter. Oh, to have one more Saxon army! There was nothing Alfred could do but return to deal with this threat. For the next six months secondary conflicts would keep him from joining Edward in the field.

But help did come to Edward. The prince had chased the Danes northward twenty miles to the banks of the Thames and then across the river into Buckinghamshire. Here they had taken refuge at Thorney, an island formed by two branches of the river Colne. Watching them from day to day, awaiting the time when they should move out of their fastness, Edward was heartened by the arrival of his brother-in-law Ethelred, ealdorman of Mercia, with troops from London.

Still, however, the Saxon forces were not strong enough to assault the island. The Danes, though, stood little chance of sallying forth without sacrificing the life of their badly wounded chieftain. This they would not do. When both sides realized that compromise was inevitable, the Saxons offered the Danes the opportunity to depart in peace if they would quit the English kingdom. Under these terms, the Danes were free to withdraw to the Danelaw, and this they did, further augmenting the formidable forces centered at Benfleet. The English lands in their path had been spared, but the Danish army had gained its objective of joining forces with Haesten.

The Saxons, however, were alert to opportunity. In the summer, when Haesten left his base for a plundering expedition in Mercia, they did not chase after him. Instead, Edward and Ethelred led about half the fyrd, the London volunteers, and recruits from the West Country in an attack on Benfleet. Haesten was missed by the camp's defenders. The English triumph was complete. Armor, cattle, and all the trophies of war were proudly borne to London. Viking ships, insofar as there were Saxon crews to man them, were rowed or sailed to London or Rochester. The others were not left to be reclaimed by their owners. With sledges, the English broke the bodies of these proud dragons and consigned them to a huge bonfire, the heads doubtless staring out wildly from the consuming flames.[4]

No Englishman could have been more exultant than Edward as he returned to his father, carrying with him the captured wife and sons of Haesten. Here were hostages that would bring the old terror to heel. But Alfred could not accept this gift of fate. He could not subject Haesten's wife to the misery of captivity. As for the two boys, one was Alfred's godson, the other Ethelred's, and the king and the ealdorman had vowed to protect both. The falsity of the husband and father could not cancel the debt of common humanity to the mother and children. Alfred sent them back to Haesten under protective escort.

When the defeated Danes were reunited with Haesten's army, the two forces moved up along the Thames, gathering reinforcements from the East Angles and Northumbrians. Behind them came Ethelred of Mercia with the ealdormen of Wilts and Somerset, together with men from virtually every burh east of the Parret and farther outposts, and recruits from North Wales. The Danes took refuge on an island in the Severn which they quickly fortified. Besieged by the English, the Danes held out until they had eaten most of their own horses and the rest had died. They then made a dash for freedom. Some by the swiftness of their flight escaped the general slaughter.

The fortunes of war now had shifted almost decisively in favor of Alfred. The Danes, however, might still gain the ascendancy by attritional assaults on the fyrd or by a bold surprise attack, or a combination of the two.

A surprise attack came while the Saxons were harvesting their crops. The hard riding Danes, who this time had left their wives and ships secure in East Anglia, dashed up the old Roman road of Watling Street and seized the deserted city of Chester before the English could catch up. They dug in behind its ancient Roman walls, the most formidable man-made barriers in England.

After futilely besieging the Danes for two days, the English once again resorted to Fabian tactics. They seized all the cattle in the area, burnt all the corn, and destroyed the pastures. This Danish campaign came to an end.

But another Danish army was active, the one which Alfred had repulsed at Exeter. It now attacked Colchester, only to be put to flight by the townsmen, who slew hundreds of them and took their ships. Alfred's burh system was proving its value.

But the defeated army was still formidable. It had moved up the Thames in its dragon ships and then up the River Lea to a point about twenty miles north of London. The city was menaced. Men from the London burh made a bold frontal assault, only to be rolled back with losses that included four king's thanes.

Alfred took personal charge of the problem. He still had a score to settle with this army of Danes. With the fyrd, the king encamped near the enemy so that his countrymen might safely harvest the crops to feed London. Meanwhile he made long reconnaissance rides through the countryside. He must have thought of the days and nights seventeen years before when his reconnaissance had been on foot across the moors and swamps of Somerset. On one of these rides by the

river, Alfred noted that the stream could be obstruct-
ed to prevent the escape of the enemy vessels. "And
then this was carried out," reports the *Chronicle* with
tantalizing taciturnity, adding only: "Two fortresses
were made on the two sides of the river."[5] According
to Henry of Huntingdon, "The king caused the waters of the Lea to be divided into three arms, that
they might not be able to convey back their ships on
it."[6] Whatever Alfred did, it was effective. When his
men had just begun their work of obstruction, "the
enemy perceived that they could not bring their ships
out."[7] Abandoning the vessels, they withdrew overland
to Bridgeworth on the Severn and there built a fortress. Exultant men from London broke up part of
the ships and returned to their city in the others.

And so, three years after returning to England for
conquest, the Great Army had to abandon its grandi-
ose dreams. England's king was aging by medieval
standards, but he still had his cunning and his daring.
And, in his eldest son and son-in-law, he had unusual-
ly able and energetic lieutenants. Most impressive of
all, thanks to Alfred's burh system, the towns were no
longer plump, soft game for marauding Vikings. The
golden dragon of Wessex was more than a match for
the hordes of lesser dragons pressing upon him.

The *Chronicle* spoke with an understatement that
was to become characteristic of English annals:

> And afterwards in the summer of this year the Dan-
> ish army divided, one force going into East Anglia and
> one into Northumbria; and those that were moneyless
> got themselves ships and went south across the sea to
> the Seine. By the grace of God, the army had not on
> the whole afflicted the English people very greatly.[8]

Though the crisis was past, the Danes continued to
wage a war of costly harassment. Marauding bands
from East Anglia and Northumbria made hit-and-run
raids on the channel coast of Wessex, escaping retri-
bution as they moved off in their swift dragon ships.
Alfred was not disposed to accept this nuisance. He
resolved to create a navy that outclassed the Viking
fleets. He had proved his talents for design in erect-

ing buildings. He now turned to naval architecture, apparently bringing to this new study the same intense concentration that he had brought to the translation of the classics. Alfred's originality is testified to by the *Chronicle*'s description of his creations: "They were built neither on the Frisian nor the Danish pattern, but as it seemed to him himself that they could be most useful."[9] No graphic representation of these ships is available today and no archaeologist has yet unearthed one of the originals. But the *Chronicle* does tell us that the new ships were almost twice as long as those of the Vikings. Some had sixty oars, some more. They were higher, steadier and swifter than their Frisian and Viking counterparts. Alfred had beaten the master shipbuilders of Europe at their own game.

They should be great battleships. The testing came when six Danish ships raided the Isle of Wight and proceeded to plunder the Devon coast. Alfred sent out nine of his new ships to challenge the raiders. The English captured two enemy vessels and were on the point of capturing a third when the king's ships ran aground. Before they could shove off, their adversaries escaped. But, as was to happen nearly seven hundred years later with the Spanish Armada, nature completed the work of destruction begun by the island's defenders. Two enemy ships were driven ashore by the wind and tide. Only one dragon ship reached the safety of East Anglia.

The running aground of Alfred's ships may have been due to a flaw in design which he later eliminated, to the inexperience of crews in handling the new vessels, or to their ignorance of the coastal waters if (as has been suggested) they were Frisian. But the fact that the enemy (great sailors manning ships of time-tested design) also ran aground suggests that weather conditions played a larger part than human frailty.

More decisive proofs of the new ships lay ahead. That summer, the *Chronicle* seems to indicate, twenty or more dragon ships were destroyed off the Wessex coast by Alfred's fleet.[10] Upon the king's adventure in shipbuilding is based the oft-asserted claim he was the

father of the English navy. Alfred's naval achievements were celebrated in 1740 in *Alfred: A Masque,* a musical entertainment from which survives one familiar song, "Rule Britannia."[11]

After 896, while Alfred was not freed from vexations in dealing with or fending off various groups of Danes, he was released from anxiety that his kingdom was in imminent peril. There was time to strengthen the reign of law of which his code was the concrete expression, time to plan further for the education of his subjects, time for the building, and the literary and philosophical studies that he loved. In the course of the day, he might settle a land dispute, translate a chapter of Latin, make by hand his own alterations in a builder's sketch of a tower, inspect one of the network of burhs still under construction, listen absorbedly to a traveler's report of distant lands, and recite Anglo-Saxon verses for an audience of family and friends. Yet, there was time for his family. He could be proud of all five of his offspring. His eldest son, Edward, had courage, intelligence, decisiveness. He would be a good king, perhaps a great one. And Alfred's son-in-law, Ethelfled's husband, Ethelred of Mercia, was as dependable a lieutenant as a king could wish.

The king took special delight in a young grandson, Edward's son Athelstan. One day Alfred "knighted" him, placing a scarlet cloak about him and fastening to his side a sword sheathed in gold.[12] The grandfather must have had in mind the time when he, as a small boy, had been similarly invested by the pope.

There is no clear record of whether the physical affliction which had tormented Alfred most of his life was eased after 893, but some think it may have been. The chief evidence, an ambiguous sentence in Asser,[13] is slender, but one would like to think that the king—who for so many years had known no day free of both pain and the threat of it—enjoyed at last the luxury of extended periods free from torment.

Alfred's writings reveal a frequent turning to thoughts of mortality not surprising in one of deep religious conviction, reared in the Middle Ages amid many dangers to life, who despite much illness had lived to mourn over the graves of three brothers, none of whom lived as long as he. He had found consolation in philosophy, but not as much as Boethius had. Nevertheless, the future of his earthly kingdom had to the last a strong claim on Alfred's thoughts and energies. In 899, he met at Chelsea with Ethelred of Mercia and Archbishop Plegmund to plan the rebuilding of London. But that project became the work of other minds and hands. On the 26th of October, 899[14], the king died.

The *Chronicle* reported:

> In this year Alfred the son of Ethelwulf died, six days before All Saints' day. He was king over the whole English people except for that part which was under Danish rule, and he had held the kingdom for one and a half years less than thirty, and then his son Edward succeeded to the kingdom.[15]

A more fitting epitaph might have been the concluding words of the great epic of that Anglo-Saxon literature that the king had loved so well. With the torches flickering around Alfred's bier as in the old great hall at Dorchester in his boyhood, a scop might have caressed the strings of his harp as in those days and chanted of a people who

> Bemoaned the fall of their mighty lord;
> Said he was kindest of earthly kings,
> Mildest, most gentle, most eager for fame.[16]

XIII

ROYAL LEGACY

lfred's will[1] is both a valuable document of English history and a fascinating confirmation of his character and personality as delineated by his earliest biographers. It is in part autobiographical, recounting how Alfred came into his inheritance, how he came without eagerness to the throne but very soon proved to the Witan in a memorable confrontation that he would be king in more than name. Equally interesting are the indirect revelations of Alfred's relationships with his family, his friends, his lieutenants temporal and spiritual, and with the humblest of his subjects. He bequeaths estates to his children and to nephews. Among those left to his wife, Ealhswith, was his birthplace at Wantage. Since the king was sentimental about his early life one is tempted to speculate about the fondness which inspired this particular bequest. Gifts of money went in equal measure to his nephews and his ealdormen with the additional gift of a valuable sword to one ealdorman, Ethelred of Mercia, the son-in-law on whose sword arm Alfred had so often relied. The king specifically repudiated any custom that might

161

prevent his leaving property to "women's hands" as
well as "weapon hands." Money was left, too, "to the
men who follow me, to whom I now give gifts at Eastertide." Other gifts went to bishops and priests. The
atmosphere of *noblesse oblige* in which Alfred was
reared is recalled by the setting aside of funds for
those poor people whom he and his father had been
accustomed to help.

But the true legacy of Alfred is of proportions that
dwarf the bequests in his will. Everywhere that the
impress of western civilization has been felt in modern
times, men and women are his legatees. His latest
beneficiaries will always be those who stand "heirs to
all the ages, foremost in the files of time."

Generations of historians, as we have seen, have
called Alfred the noblest character among statesmen
in world history. He is almost universally considered
one of the two greatest rulers of Medieval Europe, the
other being Charlemagne. But too many English and
American historians have accepted without argument
the French evaluation of Alfred as the lesser figure of
the two. Most concede to the Anglo-Saxon king superiority in character. All concede superiority in scholarship and many in native genius. It is also generally
granted that Alfred's extraordinary versatility and
wide range of interests made him much more the active molder of his people's culture than Charlemagne
was of his. But it is frequently argued that Charlemagne deserves the larger place in history because he
played his part on a larger stage—the European continent—rather than an island on the frontier of civilization. This contention ignores the perspective of
history. The sequel to the drama in which Alfred
played has had the world for its theater. Sir Arthur
Bryant concisely says of him:

> He had created two things that were to survive disas-
> ter and conquest—a kingdom to which all Englishmen
> instinctively felt they belonged and a native literature
> to enshrine their culture and tradition. More than any
> other man he was the first maker of England.[2]

Without disparaging the authentic greatness of Charlemagne, we can frankly say that his achievements have not been as enduring as Alfred's. Even before the emperor's death in 814, the forces of faction that would split his empire into warring kingdoms were already at work within his court. Under Alfred's heirs the kingdom he founded was enlarged and made a more prestigious force in world affairs. No one should minimize the importance of the "Carolingian Renaissance" but even the significance of this achievement pales before Alfred's unique accomplishment in not only making classical literature available to his people in their own language but also, in so doing, creating what is today the "largest, most varied, and oldest body of non-Latin European literature which has survived."[3] Alfred is the father of that English prose which has been the vehicle of some of the world's greatest literature and some of its most extensive commerce in both goods and ideas. It is not surprising that Alfred, himself an earnest student and translator of the classics, should have played an even larger personal role in his people's cultural revolution than the Frankish emperor who, for all his astuteness and patronage of letters, was not himself a scholar. To say that Alfred was a greater historical figure than Charlemagne is not to disparage the Holy Roman Emperor, but to indicate the stature of the English king whose contributions to civilization have proved even vaster and more durable than those of the colossus that bestrode Europe in the year 800.

Asser thought that Alfred was able to accomplish so much partly because he was fortunate in his ancestors. The durability of his contributions is equally attributable to the quality of his descendants. Alfred's immediate successor, his son Edward, was one of England's ablest rulers and one of its greatest military leaders. And Edward's spectacular success in building a united kingdom secure from the Danes was due in part to the energy, decisiveness, and diplomatic and military talents of his sister Ethelfled.[4] Alfred's policy of educating his daughters as well as his sons paid off richly for his people and in the fulfillment of his own dreams. The pages of western history may offer no parallel to the effectiveness of Edward and Ethelfled as a brother and sister team. Some years before Ethelred's death in 911, his energies had been greatly diminished, perhaps by advancing age and illnesses, and Ethelfled had assumed the leadership of Mercia in all but name. After her husband's death, she ruled in name as well as Lady of the Mercians. Alfred's son and daughter carried forward his building of burhs, he constructing at least seven in the southeast midlands, she ten in the northwest midlands. In addition she restored the defenses of Chester. She compelled Welsh acknowledgment of her suzerainty and brought Northumberland under her influence. She forged an alliance of Anglo-Danish Northumbrians, Britons, Picts, and Scots to repel Irish-Norse raids. Acknowledgment of Edward's sovereignty by one who had brought so many disparate kingdoms under her sway secured general recognition of his overlordship. Surely this remarkable woman was no less gifted in statecraft than Elizabeth I and, like her, could have claimed to have "the heart and stomach of a king, and a king of England, too."

When Edward came to the throne, the Danes still controlled East Anglia. Construction of the system of burhs was interrupted by Danish incursions from Leicester and Northampton in 913 and by a return of Vikings up the Severn the following year. Within two years, Edward had gained the upper hand in his struggle with the invaders and their island-based allies. In 917 Edward and Ethelfled launched an historic offensive that, through the sister's dramatic conquest of the mighty Danish fortress at Derby and the brother's brilliant conquest of the Cambridge area, Northampton, Huntingdon, and Colchester, brought surrender of all Danish forces in East Anglia and a few months later of all independent Danish forces in the midlands. Alfred's dream of national unity had been realized within eighteen years of his death. The achievement had come through Alfred's strategy, bril-liantly executed by his heirs. By 924 even the Irish-Norwegians had joined the English, Picts, Scots, and Northumbrian Danes in choosing Edward "for father and for lord." By now, Ethelfled had been dead for six years, but she had earned a permanent place with Edward in the history and legends of her people.

Ethelfled's influence had doubtless been strong in the upbringing of Edward's successor, his son Athelstan, who was reared at her court in Mercia. On Edward's death in 924, the beloved grandson whom Alfred had invested with the regalia of knighthood was elected king by the Mercians, preliminary to his crowning on September 4, 925 as king of all England. The first Saxon to have so all-inclusive a coronation, he emblazoned on the charters and engraved on the coins of his realm the title *rex totius Britanniae* (king of all Britain). When Scots and Danes combined against him in 937, he won at Brunanburh one of England's most celebrated victories.

With Athelstan began that influence of the House of Wessex in continental affairs that presaged the worldwide impact of Alfred's accomplishments. Alfred had created a dynasty and a nation that would help to remake western civilization. Athelstan became, in Sir Winston Churchill's words, "one of the first sovereigns of Western Europe."[5] His ties with the continent were strengthened by the marriages of his three sisters, wives respectively of Carolingian King Charles, Capetian ruler Hugh the Great, and Otto the Saxon, who would become Holy Roman emperor. He even had as his vassal Haakon the Good, king of Norway, who at the age of fifteen gained the Norwegian throne with the aid of English ships and warriors. Athelstan's nephew Louis, future king of the Franks, was reared in the Anglo-Saxon court. It was with Athelstan's aid that his own godson Alan of Brittany won back the rule of that land. In Athelstan's reign, England became much the sort of model kingdom that Alfred had envisioned. A celebrated collector of books, the grandson fostered learning as his grandsire had. He simplified Alfred's legal codes to meet the needs of an increasingly complex society and punished both arro-

gance and corruption in those who administered the
law. Far ahead of his time in humane understanding,
he mitigated the punishments for juvenile offenders.
He established uniform coinage for the entire kingdom and regulated the mints. And his accomplishments were noted in countries even more remote
from the centers of European culture than the world
of the Anglo-Saxons had been deemed when Alfred
had first come to the throne. "Now is the highest
deer-forest subject to valiant Athelstan," sang a poet
of Iceland.[6]

Athelstan was succeeded by his eighteen-year-old
brother Edmund, who had been his secundarius at
Brunanburh two years before, just as Alfred, also at
age sixteen, had served his older brother in the same
role at Ashdown. England could not have hoped for a
more effective protector than she had during the six
years of his reign.

Edmund's successor, his brother Eadred, like
Alfred, accomplished much in a life of continuous illness. Leading armies in the field despite his infirmity,
he defended the kingdom against all rebels and invaders and made Northumbria an integral part of England. So strong was the kingdom upon his death in
955 that there was no crisis when his fifteen-year-old
nephew, Eadwig, succeeded to the throne. Indeed, for
a quarter of a century the realm was not troubled by
threat of foreign invasion. When Eadwig died four
years after his coronation, much of the business of the
kingdom as well as the allegiance of many of his subjects had already passed to his brother Edgar, who
was crowned king at Bath in ceremonies that since
have attended the coronation of English monarchs into the twentieth century. Even more dramatically sym-
bolic was the fact that when the new-crowned king
sailed with his fleet up the Dee to Chester, the oars of
his royal barge were manned by eight vassal kings, including those of Scotland and Wales.[7]

Tenth century England, so largely the creation of
Alfred, had the strongest political institutions in Western Europe. In its system of taxation, of currency and

coinage, as well as in soundly based wealth, England had far outdistanced all the continental kingdoms. In effective local government and in a system of laws derived from Alfred's code, it was likewise far in advance of its European neighbors. The English system of charters was the envy of the former Carolingian empire. And the very title deeds of civilization itself were recorded by English scholars and artists in the world's most beautiful illuminated manuscripts.

So vigorous was England's culture that it flourished not only in the reigns of Edgar and Edward II, his successor, but also after the crowning of Ethelred the Unready, the only ruler of the house of Wessex to be ineffective after attaining his majority. After Ethelred's death, the old genius of Europe's noblest dynasty flared forth again in his son, Edmund Ironside. With a brilliance and daring that recalled Alfred's exploits after Athelney, the young man revitalized the kingdom while fighting off another mighty Danish invasion. But death claimed Edmund at twenty-two and Canute, "ruling sovereign of the north,"[8] claimed England. Though king as well of his native Denmark, Norway, and Scotland, Canute chose England for his home and seat of empire. In love with Anglo-Saxon civilization, he sought to become an Englishman. Ruling by—and under—Alfred's laws, he became the chief defender of Anglo-Saxon civilization. There was no trauma of transition when, upon Canute's death and the dissolution of his empire in 1035, England returned to Saxon rule. Churchill has written:

> In these days of reviving anarchy all men's minds turned to the search for some stable institution. This could only be found in monarchy, and the illustrious line of Alfred the Great possessed unequalled claims and titles. It was the Saxon monarchy which for five or six generations had provided the spearhead of resistance to the Danes. The West Saxon line was the oldest in Europe. Two generations back the house of Capet were lords of little more than Paris and the Ile de France, and the Norman dukes were Viking rovers. A sense of sanctity and awe still attached to any who could claim descent from the Great King....[9]

When in 1066 simultaneous invasion of England by
the Scandinavians and the Normans proved too much
even for English armies under the generalship of the
valiant Harold, and William the Conqueror became
the master of English soil, Anglo-Saxon culture was
never crushed. The Normans recorded their amaze-
ment at the island kingdom's wealth of art objects,
dazzling beyond anything they had seen on the continent. In this achievement, said a Norman chronicler,
England "surpassed Gaul many times over."[10]

The Normans were impressed with other accomplishments of the English. Great pragmatists, William
and his lieutenants were quick to appreciate the possibilities of the governmental machinery which they
found. In fact, research indicates that the Normans
borrowed the idea of the central treasury and national
revenue system from Anglo-Saxon England instead of
conferring it upon them as a benefit, as was once supposed.[11] And William and his successors seized eagerly
upon the English system of writs as "the most efficient
means of publishing the ruler's will which western Europe had so far known."[12] They were also happy to
copy the Anglo-Saxon coinage which had already
been imitated in Scandinavia and Italy.[13]

If mounting evidence supports Sir Alfred Clapham's statement that "in the minor arts the Norman
Conquest was little short of a catastrophe, blotting out
alike a good tradition and an accomplished execution
and setting in its place a semibarbaric art which attempted little and did that little ill,"[14] justice also compels us to repeat Professor Knowles' reminder that the
Normans "preserved, used and developed much that
was native to England."[15] We must, too, second his
praise: "They showed, indeed, a genius for strong and
intelligent rule, devoid of any overruling policy of ra-
cial aggrandizement, which must be almost unique in
Western history."[16] Commenting on this quotation,
Dorothy Whitelock says: "That the Normans are now
being commended as much for what they kept as for
what they brought may perhaps be the main result of
a generation of Anglo-Saxon studies."[17]

So vital was the Anglo-Saxon culture that it conquered England's conquerors. China's cultural conquest of its Mongol and Manchu overlords was no more thoroughgoing than England's cultural conquest of the Danes and the Normans. The English tongue, which Alfred had trained and disciplined to literary use, never died out under Norman rule. It did not even retreat to the confines of folk usage. As R.W. Chambers proved in his brilliant historical introduction to the 1932 edition of *Nicholas Harpsfield's Life of Sir Thomas More*, English literary prose persisted in an unbroken line from Alfred through the reigns of his Anglo-Saxon and Danish successors, and the generations of Norman rule, into our own time.[18] At the time of the Norman conquest, English was the Lingua Franca of Northern Europe. "There was one speech in the north," lamented the Icelandic singer of *Gunnlaugs Saga*, "before William the Bastard won England."[19] Though English would not be the language of international diplomacy again for generations, the English language continued to be written with an exactness and eloquence that would have delighted Alfred. Aelfric and Wulfstan and the anonymous northern and Canterbury chroniclers of the eleventh century wrote with memorable vividness; the Peterborough chroniclers worked into the twelfth century with plodding efficiency. Between the twelfth century and the fourteenth, when English prose again became fashionable, some of the most moving lines in English literature glowed on the pages of sermons and devotional treatises. At the end of this period, the king's English was once again the prestige speech of the land. One can only concur with Chambers: "If English prose has any known father, that father is Alfred."[20] And one must also agree when he says "it is undeniable that, after a long struggle what comes at last to the top is not merely the English language, but essentially an English, not a French, civilization; an English mind, not a French."[21]

The heritage from Alfred, in the political institutions and the language to which he gave form, is con-

169

tinuous into the twentieth century. "That great king,"
wrote W.P. Ker, "has been frequently threatened with
ostracism, yet neither the political nor the literary history can do without him, and the literary like the political history of England is continuous."[22]

Continuous and broadening, he might have said. It
is an interesting curiosity of history that in England's
great Elizabethan age, both the queen herself and the
greatest creative genius of the era, William Shakespeare, were lineal descendants of Alfred.[23] It is equally curious that in the mighty Victorian age, both the
queen and her greatest prime minister, William Ewart
Gladstone, were also lineal descendants of Alfred.[24]
And it is perhaps no less remarkable that when a battle for the rights of Englishmen that was to create a
great western republic began an ocean away from the
island where those rights were first enunciated, the
general of the new nation's armies and its first magis-
trate was George Washington, another lineal descendant of Alfred the Great.[25] But, even had there been
no genetic link between these famous people and the
Saxon king, they would still have been his heirs. For
they spoke and wrote a language that would not have
been theirs but for Alfred, and they were the prod-
ucts of a culture that would not have survived the vi-
cissitudes of war except for the great king's successful
defense of his land and infusion of his own enthusiastic spirit into every aspect of its civilization.
"Throughout a third of the earth's habitable surface
the forms of government and law which men practice
are based on forms of government and law evolved in
England"[26]—an entity that owes its existence to Alfred
more than to anyone else in human history. And the
influence of that culture on other civilizations—like
their influence in turn on English culture—is incalculable.

Reason enough, surely, for Alfred's career to be a
matter of interest to every inhabitant of the globe with
an intelligent curiosity about the sources of his civilization. But there is another reason for interest, one having to do even more with the future than the past. In

his monumental *A Study of History* with its survey of twenty-one civilizations, Arnold Toynbee has concluded that their survival or demise has been largely a matter of challenge and response. Without challenge there is decay. Without vigorous and effective response, there is destruction. As one of the most striking examples of a people's successful response to fearful challenge, Toynbee cites the experience of Wessex under Alfred: "At that stage it looked as though the future lay, not with Wessex, but with Mercia. In the ninth century, however, when the challenge from the Celtic fringe was outclassed by a new and far more formidable challenge from Scandinavia, these prospects were falsified. This time Mercia failed to respond, while Wessex under the leadership of Alfred responded triumphantly and thereby became the nucleus of the historic Kingdom of England."[27]

Charles Plummer wrote: "Every historian is agreed that this is the turning-point in the history, not only of England, but of Western Europe." And he reenforced his statement with a quotation from John Richard Green:

> "Wessex was saved; and in saving Wessex, Alfred saved England; and in saving England, he saved Western Europe from becoming a heathen Scandinavian power."[28]

There will always be a lesson for humankind in the life of the man who did not concede defeat when his kingdom was reduced to thirty acres in a swamp and he himself had become a fugitive, who could overcome barbarism without becoming barbaric, who despite his triumphs in war was always prouder of his victories for peace, and who, though he made his kingdom the wealthiest in Europe, was ever mindful that poverty dwells where there are no riches of mind and spirit. Amid all the tarnished standards of famous leaders—emblems that, upon close scrutiny, seem to fade before the eye seeking to descry dark upon dark—an occasional ensign stands forth in undimmed luster as a rallying point in the gloom. Not least among these is the Golden Dragon of Wessex.

APPENDICES

ALFRED'S LAW

Now I, King Alfred, have collected these laws, and have given orders for copies to be made of many of those which our predecessors observed and which I myself approved of. But many of those I did not approve of I have annulled, by the advice of my councillors, while [in other cases] I have ordered changes to be introduced. For I have not dared to presume to set down in writing many of my own, for I cannot tell what [innovations of mine] will meet with the approval of our successors. But those which were the most just of the laws I found—whether they dated from the time of Ine my kinsman, or of Offa, king of the Mercians, or of AEthelberht, who was the first [king] to be baptised in England—these I have collected while rejecting the others.

I, then, Alfred, King of the West Saxons, have shewn these to all my councillors, and they have declared that it met with the approval of all, that they should be observed.

1. In the first place we enjoin you, as a matter of supreme importance, that every man shall abide carefully by his oath and his pledge.

   §1. If anyone is wrongfully constrained to promise either of these: to betray his lord or to render aid in an unlawful undertaking, then it is better to be false [to the promise] than to perform it.

   §2. If, however, he pledges himself to something which it is lawful to carry out and proves false to his pledge, he shall humbly give his weapons and possessions to his friends to keep, and remain 40 days in prison at a royal manor, and undergo there whatever [sentence] the bishop prescribes for him; and his relatives shall feed him if he himself has no food.

From F. L. Attenborough: *The Laws of the Earliest English Kings*. Reprinted by permission of Cambridge University Press.

§3. If he has no relatives, and [if he] has not the [necessary] food, the king's reeve shall provide him with it.

§4. If he will not submit unless force is used against him, [i.e.] if he has to be bound, he shall forfeit his weapons and his property.

§5. If he is slain, no wergeld shall be paid for him.

§6. If he runs away before the term [of imprisonment is completed] and is recaptured, he shall remain in prison 40 days, as he ought to have done at first.

§7. If he succeeds in making his escape, he shall be banished, and excommunicated from all the churches of Christ.

§8. If, however, other men stand surety for him, he shall pay the compensation [due to them] for violation of bail, as the law directs him, and the compensation for breach of faith, as his confessor prescribes for him.

2. If a man flees, for any manner of offence, to any monastery which is entitled to receive the king's food, rent, or to any other free community which is endowed, for the space of three days he shall have right of asylum, unless he is willing to come to terms [with his enemy].

§1. If, during that time, anyone injures him by a [mortal] blow, [by putting him in] fetters, or by wounding him, he shall pay compensation for each of these offences in the regular way, both with wergeld and fine, and he shall pay 120 shillings to the community as compensation for violation of the sanctuary of the Church, and he [himself] shall not have the payment due to him from the fugitive.

3. If anyone violates the king's protection, he shall pay compensation for the crime [to the injured person], as the law directs him, and 5 pounds of pure silver pennies for violation of the king's protection; for violation of the archbishop's protection or guardianship 3 pounds must be paid as compensation; for violation of the protection or the guardianship of any other bishop or of an *ealdorman* 2 pounds must be paid as compensation.

4. If anyone plots against the life of the king, either on his own account, or by harbouring outlaws, or men belonging to [the king] himself, he shall forfeit his life and all he possesses.

§1. If he wishes to clear himself [from such a charge), he shall do it by an oath equal to the king's wergeld.

§2. And likewise with regard to all classes, both commoners and nobles, we ordain; he who plots against the life of his lord shall forfeit his life to him, and all he possesses, or he shall clear himself by [an oath equal to] his lord's wergeld.

5. Further, we grant to every church consecrated by a bishop this right of sanctuary: if a man, attacked by enemies, reaches it either on foot or on horseback, he shall not be dragged out for seven days, if he can live despite hunger, and unless he [himself comes] out [and] fights. If, however, anyone does try to drag him out, he shall forfeit the amount due for violation of the king's guardianship and the fine for violating the sanctuary of the church—and a greater amount if he seizes more than one person in such a place.

§1. If the community have so great need of their church [that it cannot be used as an asylum], he [the fugitive] shall be kept in another building, and this shall not have more doors than the church.

§2. The chief authority of the church shall see to it, that during this time no food is given to him.

§3. If he himself is willing to hand over his weapons to his enemies, they shall hold him in their power for thirty days; and they shall send formal notice of his position to his kinsmen.

§4. The privilege of sanctuary belonging to a church includes also the following: if anyone takes refuge in a church, because of any offence which up to that time had been kept secret, and there confesses his sin in God's name, half the punishment shall be remitted him.

§5. We decree that he who steals on Sunday, or during Christmas or Easter, or on Holy Thursday, at Rogation Days, shall pay in each case double compensation, just as he must [if he steals] during Lent.

6. If anyone steals anything from a church, he shall pay the value of the article and the fine which is appropriate to the value in question, and the hand shall be struck off which committed the theft.

§1. If he wishes to redeem his hand, and if it is decided to give him permission to do so, he shall pay [such fine] as is appropriate to his wergeld.

7. If anyone fights or draws his weapon in the king's hall, and [if he] is arrested, it shall be for the king to decide whether he shall be put to death, or permitted to live, in case the king is willing to forgive him .

§1. If he escapes and is subsequently arrested, he shall pay for himself by his wergeld in every case; and he shall pay compensation for the offence—both wergeld and fine—according to the nature of the outrage he has perpetrated.

8. If anyone takes a nun from a nunnery without the permission of the king or bishop, he shall pay 120 shillings, half to the king, and half to the bishop and the lord of the church, under whose charge the nun is.

§1. If she lives longer than he who abducted her, she shall inherit nothing of his property.

§2. If she bears a child, it shall inherit no more of the property than its mother.

§3. If her child is slain, the share of the wergeld due to the mother's kindred shall be paid to the king, but the father's kindred shall be paid the share due to them.

9. If anyone slays a woman with child, while the child is in her womb, he shall pay the full wergeld for the woman, and half the wergeld for the child, [which shall be] in accordance with the wergeld of the father's kindred.

§1. Until the value amounts to 30 shillings, the fine shall be 60 shillings in every case. When the [said] value amounts to this sum, the fine shall be 120 shillings.

§2. Formerly the fines to be paid by those who stole gold and horses and bees, and many other fines, were greater than the rest. Now all fines, with the exception of that for stealing men, are alike—120 shillings.

10. If anyone lies with the wife of a man whose wergeld is 1200 shillings, he shall pay 120 shillings compensation to the husband; to a husband whose wergeld is 600 shillings, he shall pay 100 shillings compensation; to a commoner he shall pay 40 shillings compensation [for a similar offence].

11. If anyone seizes by the breast a young woman belonging to the commons, he shall pay her 5 shillings compensation.

§1. If he throws her down but does not lie with her, he shall pay [her] 10 shillings compensation.

§2. If he lies with her, he shall pay [her] 60 shillings compensation.

§3. If another man has previously lain with her, then the compensation shall be half this [amount].

§4. If she is accused [of having previously lain with a man], she shall clear herself by [an oath of] 60 hides, or lose half the compensation due to her.

§5. If this [outrage] is done to a woman of higher birth, the compensation to be paid shall increase according to the wergeld.

12. If one man burns or fells the trees of another, without permission [to do so], he shall pay 5 shillings for each big tree, and 5 pence for each of the rest, however many there may be; and [he shall pay] 30 shillings as a fine .

13. If one man kills another unintentionally, [by allowing a tree to fall on him] while they are engaged on a common task, the tree shall be given to the [dead man's] kindred, and they shall remove it within 30 days from the locality. Otherwise, it shall be taken by him who owns the wood.

14. If anyone is born dumb or deaf, so that he can neither deny nor confess his wrongdoings, his father shall pay compensation for his misdeeds.

15. If anyone fights, or draws his weapon in the presence of the archbishop, he shall pay 150 shillings compensation; if this happens in the presence of another bishop or of an *ealdorman*, he shall pay 100 shillings compensation.

16. If anyone steals a cow or a broodmare, and drives off a foal or a calf, he shall pay for the latter a shilling, and for the mothers according to their value.

17. If anyone entrusts a [child or other] helpless person who is dependent on him to another, and the person accepting the charge causes the death of the person committed to him, he who nurtured him shall clear himself of criminal intention, if anyone prefers such an accusation against him.

18. If anyone lustfully seizes a nun, either by her clothes or by her breast, without her permission, he shall pay as

compensation twice the sum we have fixed in the case of a woman belonging to the laity.

§1. If a young woman who is betrothed commits fornication, she shall pay compensation to the amount of 60 shillings to the surety [of the marriage], if she is a commoner. This sum shall be [paid] in livestock, cattle being the property tendered, and no slave shall be given in such a payment.

§2. If her wergeld is 600 shillings, she shall pay 100 shillings to the surety [of the marriage].

§3. If her wergeld is 1200 shillings, she shall pay 120 shillings to the surety [of the marriage].

19. If anyone lends a weapon of his to another [man], for the purpose of committing murder with it, they may, if they are willing to, combine to pay the wergeld.

§1. If they do not combine [voluntarily], he who lent the weapon shall pay one-third of the wergeld and one-third of the fine.

§2. If he wishes to clear himself, [by swearing] he was cognisant of no criminal intention when he made the loan, he may do so.

§3. If a sword-furbisher receives a weapon or a smith receives a tool belonging to another man in order to refurbish it, in either case the article shall be returned in as good condition as that in which it has been received, unless it has been stipulated that there shall be no liability on the part of the said furbisher for damage done to it.

20. If property is entrusted to a monk in the service of another man without the permission of the monk's lord, and he loses it, its former owner shall bear the loss.

21. If a priest slays another man, he and all the share of the monastic property which he has bought for himself shall be given up; and the bishop shall unfrock him when he is ejected from the monastery and given up, unless the lord [of the monastery] is willing to answer for the wergeld [of the slain man].

22. If anyone makes an accusation [against another] at a public meeting, in the presence of the king's reeve, and afterwards wishes to withdraw it, he shall prefer the charge, if he can, against a more likely person. If he cannot he shall lose the value due to him.

23. If a dog tears or bites a man, 6 shillings shall be paid

for the first offence. If its owner continues to keep it, 12 shillings shall be paid for the second offence, and 30 shillings for the third.

§1. If the dog disappears after committing any of these offences, this compensation must nevertheless be paid.

§2. If the dog commits more offences and he [its master] still keeps it, he must pay compensation for whatsoever wounds may be inflicted, according to the amount of the [injured man's] full wergeld.

24. If a beast injures a man, [its owner] must hand over the beast [to the injured man], or come to terms [with him].

25. If anyone rapes the slave of a commoner, he shall pay 5 shillings to the commoner, and a fine of 60 shillings.

§1. If a slave rapes a slave, castration shall be required as compensation.

26. If one of a band of marauders slays an unoffending man, whose wergeld is 200 shillings, he who acknowledges the blow shall pay the wergeld and the fine; and everyone engaged in the affair shall pay 30 shillings compensation for belonging to such a band.

27. If the slain man's wergeld is 600 shillings, each man shall pay 60 shillings for belonging to such a band; and the homicide [shall pay] the wergeld and the full fine.

28. If the wergeld of the slain man is 1200 shillings, each of them [shall pay] 120 shillings; and the homicide [shall pay] the wergeld and the fine.

§1. If a band of marauders acts thus and afterwards wishes to deny it, they shall all be accused, and then all collectively shall pay the wergeld and one fine—whichever is appropriate to the wergeld.

29. If anyone rapes a girl who is not of age, the same compensation shall be paid to her as is paid to an adult.

30. If anyone who has no paternal relatives fights and kills a man, his maternal relatives, if he has any, shall pay one-third of the wergeld and his associates shall pay one-third. In default of payment of the [remaining] third, he shall be held personally responsible.

§1. If he has no maternal relatives, his associates shall pay half [the wergeld], and in default of payment of the [other] half, he shall be held personally responsible.

31. If a man in this position is slain—if he has no relatives—half the wergeld shall be paid to the king, and half to his associates.

32. If anyone utters a public slander, and it is proved against him, he shall make amends on no lighter terms than the excision of his tongue, [with the provision that] it shall not be ransomed at a cheaper price than [its value], estimated according to the [man's] wergeld.

33. If one man charges another respecting a solemn pledge given under the sanction of God, and wishes to accuse him of neglecting to perform any [one] of the promises which he has made to him, he shall pronounce the oath [of accusation] in four churches, and the other [the defendant], if he wishes to clear himself, shall do so in twelve churches.

34. Further, with regard to traders, it is decreed: they shall bring before the king's reeve, at a public meeting, the men they are taking with them up into the country, and declare how many of them there are; and they shall take with them [only] such men as they can bring to justice again, at a public meeting. And when they need to have more men with them on their journey, a similar declaration shall always be made to the king's reeve, before the assembled company, as often as need arises.

35. If anyone lays bonds on an unoffending commoner, he shall pay 10 shillings compensation.
    §1. If anyone scourges him, he shall pay 20 shillings compensation.
    §2. If he places him in the stocks, he shall pay 30 shillings compensation.
    §3. If he cuts his hair to insult him, in such a way as to spoil his appearance, he shall pay 10 shillings compensation.
    §4. If he cuts his hair after the fashion of a priest's without binding him, he shall pay 30 shillings compensation.
    §5. If he cuts off his beard, he shall pay 20 shillings compensation.
    §6. If he lays bonds on him, and then cuts his hair after the fashion of a priest's, he shall pay 60 shillings compensation.

36. It is further enacted: if a man has a spear over his shoulder, and anyone is transfixed thereon, he shall pay the wergeld without the fine.

§1. If [the man] is transfixed before his eyes, he shall pay the wergeld; and if he is accused of deliberate intention in the act, he shall clear himself with an oath equal to the fine, and thereby dismiss the claim for the fine,

§2. supposing the point to be higher than the [other] end of the shaft, by the width of three fingers. If they are both on a level, the point and the [other] end of the shaft, the man with the spear shall not be regarded as responsible for causing danger.

37. If a man wishes [to go] from one district, to seek service in another, he shall do it with the cognisance of the *ealdorman,* to whose jurisdiction he has previously been subject.

§1. If he does so without his cognisance, he who takes him into his employment shall pay a fine of 120 shillings; but he shall divide the payment, [paying] half to the king in the district where the man has been residing, and half in that to which he has come.

§2. If he has committed any manner of offence in the place where he has been [residing], he who now takes him into his employment shall pay compensation for it, and a fine of 120 shillings to the king.

38. If anyone fights at a meeting in the presence of an *ealdorman* of the king, he shall pay as compensation [such] wergeld and fine as is due, but previous to this [he shall pay] a fine of 120 shillings to the *ealdorman.*

§1. If he disturbs the meeting by drawing his weapon, he shall pay a fine of 120 shillings to the *ealdorman.*

§2. If anything of this kind takes place in the presence of an official subordinate to an *ealdorman* of the king, [or in the presence of] a king's priest, he shall pay a fine of 30 shillings.

39. If anyone fights in the house of a commoner, he shall pay the commoner 6 shillings compensation.

§1. If he draws his weapon, but does not fight, the [compensation] shall be half this sum.

§2. If either of these [offences] occurs in the house of a man whose wergeld is 600 shillings, the compensation shall be increased to three times that due to a commoner; if in the house of a man whose wergeld is 1200 shillings, [it shall be increased] to twice the compensation due to a man whose wergeld is 600 shillings.

40. The fine for breaking into the fortified premises of the king shall be 120 shillings; into those of an archbishop, 90 shillings; into those of another bishop or of an *ealdorman,* 60 shillings; into those of a man whose wergeld is 1200 shillings, 30 shillings; into those of a man whose wergeld is 600 shillings, 15 shillings. The fine for breaking through a commoner's fence shall be 5 shillings.

§1. If any of these offences occur while the army is in the field, or during the fast of Lent, the compensation [to be paid] shall be double [the above].

§2. If anyone, without permission, publicly disregards the laws of the Church during Lent, he shall pay 120 shillings compensation.

41. We have further established, that a man who holds land by title-deed, which his kinsmen have left him, shall not be allowed to give it out of his kindred, if there is documentary or [other] evidence that the power to do so is forbidden him by the men who first acquired it, or by those who gave it to him. [And he who contests such an alienation] shall make a declaration to this effect in the presence of his kindred, with the king and bishop as witnesses.

42. Also we enjoin, that a man who knows his adversary to be residing at home, shall not have recourse to violence before demanding justice of him.

§1. If he has power enough to surround his adversary and besiege him in his house, he shall keep him therein seven days, but he shall not fight against him if he [his adversary] will consent to remain inside [his residence]. And if, after seven days, he will submit and hand over his weapons, he shall keep him unscathed for thirty days, and send formal notice of his position to his kinsmen and friends.

§2. If, however, he flees to a church, the privileges of the church shall be respected, as we have declared above.

§3. If, however, he has not power enough to besiege him in his house, he shall ride to the *ealdorman* and ask him for help. If he will not help him, he shall ride to the king before having recourse to violence.

§4. And further, if anyone chances on his enemy, not having known him to be at home, and if he will give up his weapons, he shall be detained for thirty days, and his friends shall be informed [of his position]. If he is not willing to give up his weapons, then violence may be used against him. If he is willing to surrender and hand over his weapons, and anyone after that uses violence against him [the pursuer], he shall pay any sum which he incurs, whether wergeld or compensation for wounds, as well as a fine, and his kinsman shall forfeit his claim to protection as a result of his action.

§5. We further declare that a man may fight on behalf of his lord, if his lord is attacked, without becoming liable to vendetta. Under similar conditions a lord may fight on behalf of his man.

§6. In the same way a man may fight on behalf of one who is related to him by blood, if he is attacked unjustly, except it be against his lord. This we do not permit.

§7. A man may fight, without becoming liable to vendetta, if he finds another [man] with his wedded wife, within closed doors or under the same blanket; or [if he finds another man] with his legitimate daughter [or sister]; or with his mother, if she has been given in lawful wedlock to his father.

43. The following days shall be granted [as holidays] to all free men, though not to slaves and hired labourers: twelve days at Christmas and the day on which Christ overcame the devil; the anniversary of St Gregory; seven days before Easter and seven days after; one day at the festival of St Peter and St Paul, and in autumn, the full week before St Mary's mass; and one day at the celebration of All Saints. The four Wednesdays in the four Ember weeks shall be granted [as holidays] to all slaves whose chief desire is to sell anything which has been given to them in God's name, or which they are able to acquire by their labour in any portions of time at their disposal.

44. 30 shillings shall be given as compensation for a wound on the head, if both bones are pierced.
    §1. If the outer bone [only] is pierced, 15 shillings shall be given as compensation.

45. If a wound an inch long is inflicted under the hair, one shilling shall be given as compensation.
    §1. If a wound an inch long is inflicted in front of the hair, 2 shillings [shall be paid] as compensation.

46. If either ear is struck off, 30 shillings shall be given as compensation.
    §1. If the hearing is stopped, so that he cannot hear, 60 shillings shall be given as compensation.

47. If anyone knocks out a man's eye, he shall give him 66 shillings, 6 pence and the third part of a penny as compensation.
    §1. If it remains in the head, but he can see nothing with it, one-third of the compensation shall be withheld.

48. If anyone strikes off another's nose, he shall pay him 60 shillings compensation.

49. If anyone knocks out another's front tooth, he shall pay 8 shillings as compensation for it.
    §1. If it is a back tooth [that is knocked out], 4 shillings shall be given as compensation.
    §2. A man's canine tooth shall be valued at 15 shillings.

50. If anyone strikes another's jaws so violently that they are fractured, he shall pay 15 shillings compensation.
    §1. If a man's chin-bone is broken in two, 12 shillings shall be given as compensation.

51. If a man's throat is pierced, 12 shillings be paid as compensation.

52. If, as the result of another's actions, a man's tongue is torn from his mouth, the compensation [to be paid] shall be the same as that for an eye.

53. If a man is wounded in the shoulder, so that the synovia flows out, 30 shillings shall be paid as compensation.

54. If the arm is fractured above the elbow, 15 shillings must be paid as compensation for it.

55. If both bones in the arm are broken, the compensation [to be paid] shall be 30 shillings.

56. If the thumb is struck off, 30 shillings must be paid as compensation for it.

§1. If the nail is struck off, 5 shillings must be paid as compensation for it.

57. If the first finger is struck off, the compensation [to be paid] shall be 15 shillings; for the nail of the same, 3 shillings [compensation shall be paid].

58. If the middle finger is struck off, the compensation [to be paid] shall be 12 shillings; for the nail of the same, 2 shillings compensation shall be paid.

59. If the third finger is struck off, 17 shillings must be paid as compensation for it; and for the nail of the same, 4 shillings [must be paid] as compensation.

60. If the little finger is struck off, 9 shillings must be paid as compensation for it, and one shilling [must be paid as compensation for] the nail of the same, if it is struck off.

61. If a man is wounded in the belly, 30 shillings shall be given to him as compensation.

§1. If he is pierced right through, 20 shillings [shall be paid as compensation] for each orifice.

62. If a man's thigh is pierced, 30 shillings shall be given to him as compensation.

§1. If it is fractured, 30 shillings shall also be the compensation [to be paid].

63. If the shin is pierced below the knee, 12 shillings must be paid as compensation for it.

§1. If it is fractured below the knee, 30 shillings shall be given to him as compensation.

64. If the big toe is struck off, 20 shillings shall be given to him as compensation.

§1. If it is the second toe [which is struck off], 15 shillings shall be given to him as compensation.

§2. If the middle toe is struck off, 9 shillings must be paid as compensation for it.

§3. If it is the fourth toe [which is struck off], 6 shillings must be paid as compensation for it.

§4. If the little toe is struck off, 5 shillings shall be given to him [as compensation].

65. If a man is so badly wounded in the testicles that he cannot beget children, 80 shillings shall be paid to him as compensation for it.

66. If a man's arm, with the hand and all below the elbow, is cut off, 80 shillings shall be paid as compensation for it.

§1. For every wound in front of the hair, and below the sleeve and beneath the knee, the compensation shall be doubled.

67. If the loin be maimed, 60 shillings must be paid as compensation for it.

§1. If it is pierced, 15 shillings shall be given as compensation.

§2. If it is pierced right through, then 30 shillings must be paid as compensation for it.

68. If a man is wounded in the shoulder, 80 shillings shall be paid as compensation, if he continues to live.

69. If a man maims another's hand outwardly, 20 shillings shall be given to him as compensation, if he can be cured.

§1. If half of it comes off, then 40 shillings must be paid as compensation.

70. If one man breaks another's rib without breaking the skin, 10 shillings shall be given [to him] as compensation.

§1. If the skin is broken and a bone is removed, 15 shillings shall be given [to him] as compensation.

71. If a man's eye is knocked out, or if his hand or foot is struck off, the same compensation shall follow them all—6 pennies, 66 shillings and the third part of a penny.

72. If a man's shin is struck off at the knee, 80 shillings must be paid as compensation for it.

73. If anyone smashes another's shoulder, 20 shillings shall be given to him as compensation.

74. If anyone hacks into it [the shoulder], and a bone is removed, 15 shillings shall be given as compensation to it in addition to the above].

75. If the large sinew is damaged, and if it can be treated medically so as to make it sound, 12 shillings shall be given as compensation.

§1. If the man becomes lame as a result of the damage to the sinew, and if he cannot be cured, 30 shillings shall be given [to him] as compensation.

76. If the small sinew [of a man] be damaged, 6 shillings shall be given to him as compensation.

77. If one man damages the tendons in another's neck, and wounds him so severely that he has no control over them, but [if] nevertheless he continues to live so wounded, 100 shillings shall be given to him as compensation, unless the councillors award him a juster and a greater sum.

ALFRED'S WILL

I, King Alfred, by the grace of God and on consultation with Archbishop Ethelred and with the witness of all the councillors of the West Saxons, have been inquiring about the needs of my soul and about my inheritance which God and my ancestors gave to me, and about the inheritance which my father, King AEthelwulf, bequeathed to us three brothers, AEthelbald, Ethelred and myself; that whichever of us should live longest was to succeed to the whole. But it happened that AEthelbald died; and Ethelred and I, with the witness of all the councillors of the West Saxons, entrusted our share to our kinsman King Ethelbert, on condition that he should return it to us as fully at our disposal as it was when we entrusted it to him; and he then did so, both that inheritance, and what he had obtained from the use of the property we two held jointly, and what he had himself acquired.

Then it so happened that Ethelred succeeded, and I asked him in the presence of all the councillors that we might divide that inheritance and he should give me my share. He then told me that he could not divide it easily, for he had very often before attempted it; and he said that he would leave after his death to no person sooner than to me whatever he held of our joint property and whatever he acquired. And I gave a ready assent to that. But it happened that we were all harassed by the heathen army; then we spoke about our children, that they would require some property, whatever might happen to the two of us in those troubles. Then we were at an assembly at *Swinbeorg* and we then agreed in the witness of the councillors of the West Saxons that whichever of us should live longer should grant to the other's children the lands which we had ourselves obtained and the lands which King AEthelwulf gave to us in AEthelbald's lifetime, except those which he bequeathed to us three brothers. And each of us gave to the other his pledge, that whichever of us lived longer should succeed both to lands and treasures and to all the other's possessions except the part which each of us had bequeathed to his children.

English Historical Documents c. 500-1042., Vol. I. Edited by Dorothy Whitelock. New York: Oxford University Press, 1955. Reprinted by permission of the publisher.

But it happened that King Ethelred died. Then no one
made known to me any will or any testimony that the position was any other than as we had both agreed with witness. When we now heard many disputes about the
inheritance, I brought King AEthelwulf's will to our assembly at *Langanden* and it was read before all the councillors
of the West Saxons. When it had been read, I begged them
all for love of me—and offered them my pledge that I
would never bear any of them a grudge because they declared what was right—that none of them would hesitate either for love or fear of me to pronounce the common law,
lest any man should say that I wronged my young kinsfolk,
the older or the younger. And then they all rightly pronounced and declared that they could not conceive any juster title nor hear of one in the will. "Now that everything in
it has come into your possession, bequeath it and give it into the hand of kinsman or stranger, whichever you prefer."
And they all gave me their pledge and signature that as
long as they lived no man should ever change it in any way
other than as I myself bequeath it at my last day.

I, Alfred, king of the West Saxons, by the grace of God
and with this witness, declare how I wish to dispose of my
inheritance after my death. First, I grant to Edward my
elder son the land at Stratton in Trigg and Hartland and
all the booklands which Leofheah holds, and the land at
Carhampton and at Kilton and at Burnham and at Wedmore—and I beseech the community at Cheddar to choose
him on the terms which we have already agreed on—along
with the land at Chewton and what belongs to it. And I
grant him the land at Cannington and at Bedwyn and at
Pewsey and at Hurstbourne and at Sutton and at Leather-
head and at Alton.

And all the booklands which I have in Kent and at the
lower Hurstbourne and at Chiseldon are to be given to
Winchester on the terms on which my father bequeathed it,
and my private property which I entrusted to Ecgwulf at
the lower Hurstbourne.

And to my younger son the land at Arreton and that at
Dean and that at Meon and at Amesbury and at Dean
and at Sturminster and at Yeovil and at Crewkerne and
at Whitchurch and at Axmouth and at Branscombe and
at Cullompton and at Tiverton and at Milborne and at
Exminster and at *Suoeswyroe* and at Lifton, and the lands
which belong to it, namely all that I have in Cornwall
except Trigg.

And to my eldest daughter the residence at Wellow; and to my middle daughter that at Kingsclere and at Candover; and to the youngest the estate at Wellow and at Ashton and at Chippanham. And to my brother's son AEthelhelm the estate at Aldingbourne and at Compton and at Crondall and at Beeding and at Beddingham and at Burnham and at Thunderfield and at Eashing. And to my brother's son AEthelwold the residence at Godalming and at Guildford and at Steyning. And to my kinsman Osferth the residence at Beckley and at Rotherfield and at Ditchling and at Sutton and at Lyminster and at Angmering and at Felpham, and the lands which belong thereto. And to Ealhswith the estate at Lambourn and at Wantage and at Edington.

And to my two sons 1,000 pounds, 500 pounds to each; and to my eldest daughter and my middle daughter and the youngest and to Ealhswith, 400 pounds to the four of them, 100 pounds to each. And to each of my ealdormen 100 mancuses, and likewise to AEthelhelm and AEthelwold and Osferth; and to Ealdorman Ethelred a sword worth 100 mancuses. And the men who serve me, to whom I have now given money at Eastertide, are to be given 200 pounds, and it is to be divided among them, to each as much as will fall to him according to the manner in which I have just now made my distribution. And to the archbishop 100 mancuses and to Bishop Esne and to Bishop Waerferth and to the bishop of Sherborne. And there is to be distributed for me and for my father and for the friends for whom he used to intercede and I intercede, 200 pounds, 50 to priests throughout my kingdom, 50 to poor servants of God, 50 to poor men in need, 50 to the church in which I shall be buried. I know not for certain whether there is so much money, nor do I know if there is more, but I think so. If there is more, it is to be shared among all to whom I have bequeathed money; and it is my will that my ealdormen and my officials shall all be included and shall distribute it

Now I had previously written differently about my inheritance when I had property and more kinsmen, and I had entrusted the documents to many men, and in these same men's witness they were written. Therefore, I have now burnt all the old ones which I could discover. If any one of them shall be found, it has no validity, for it is my will that now it shall be as here stated, with God's help.

And it is my will that the men who hold those lands shall observe the directions which stand in my father's will to the best of their power. And if I have any unpaid debt to any one, I desire that my kinsmen certainly pay it. And it is my will that the men to whom I have bequeathed my booklands shall not give it away from my kindred after their death, but I wish that after their death it shall pass to my nearest of kin unless any of them have children; in that case I prefer that it should pass to the child born on the male side as long as any is worthy of it. My grandfather had bequeathed his land in the male line and not in the female line. If then I have given to anyone on the female side what he acquired, my kinsmen are to buy it back, if they wish to have it during their lifetime. If not, let it go after their death as we have already stated. For this reason I say that they are to pay for it, that they succeed to my lands, which I may give on the female as well as the male side, whichever I choose.

And I pray in the name of God and of his saints that none of my kinsmen or heirs oppress any of the dependents whom I have supported. And the councillors of the West Saxons pronounced it right for me to leave them free or servile, whichever I choose; but I desire for the love of God and the good of my soul that they shall be entitled to their freedom and free choice. And I command in the name of the living God that no one is to harass them either by demands of money or by any thing, so that they may not choose such lord as they wish. And I desire that the community at Damarham be given their title-deeds and freedom to choose whatever lord they prefer, both for my sake and for AElfflaed and for the friends for whom she used to intercede and I intercede. And from my livestock let such payment be made for the good of my soul as is possible and is also fitting and as you wish to give on my behalf.

BIBLIOGRAPHY

Adams, J. Q. *A Life of William Shakespeare.* Boston: Houghton Mifflin Co., 1923.

The Anglo-Saxon Chronicle. Revised translation edited by Dorothy Whitelock *et al.* New Brunswick, New Jersey: Rutgers University Press, 1961.

Asser's Life of King Alfred. Edited with Introduction and Commentary by William Henry Stevenson. Includes article by Dorothy Whitelock on recent criticism of *Asser's Life of Alfred.* Oxford: The Clarendon Press, 1959.

Barraclough, Geoffrey. *The Medieval Papacy.* New York: Harcourt, Brace & World, Inc., 1968.

Bately, Janet M. "Grimbald of St. Bertin's." *Medium AEvum,* XXXV (1966), pp. 1-10.

_____ "King Alfred and the Old English Translation of Orosius." *Anglia,* LXXXVIII (1970), pp. 433-460.

_____ "The Relationship between Geographical Information in the Old English Orosius and Latin Texts Other than Orosius." *Anglo Saxon England,* Vol. I, Ed. Peter Clemoes. Cambridge: University Press, 1973.

Blair, Peter Hunter. *An Introduction to Anglo-Saxon England.* Cambridge: The University Press, 1962.

_____. *Roman Britain and Early England, 55 B.C.—A.D. 871.* Vol. I of *A History of England.* Edited by Christopher Brooke and Denis Mack Smith. Edinburgh: Thomas Nelson and Sons, Ltd., 1963.

Brooke, Christopher. *From Alfred to Henry III, 871-1272.* Vol. II of *A History of England.* Edited by Christopher Brooke and Denis Mack Smith. Edinburgh: Thomas Nelson and Sons, Ltd., 1961.

Brown, William H., Jr. *A Syntax of King Alfred's Pastoral Care.* The Hague: Mouton, 1970.

Bruce-Mitford, R.L.S. (ed.). *Recent Archaeological Excavations in Britain.* London: Routledge & Kegan Paul, 1956.

Bryant, Sir Arthur. *Makers of England.* Formerly titled *The Story of England: Makers of the Realm.* New York: Doubleday & Company, Inc., 1962.

Cam, Helen. *Law-Finders and Law-Makers in Medieval England: Collected Studies in Legal and Constitutional History.* New York: Barnes & Noble, Inc., 1962.

Campbell, Alistair (ed.), *The Tollemache Orosius (British Museum Original Ms. 47967).* Early English Manuscripts in Facsimile, Vol. III. Copenhagen: Rosenkilde and Bagger, 1953.

Carnicelli, Thomas A. (ed.), *King Alfred's Version of St. Augustine's Soliloquies.* Cambridge, Mass., Harvard University Press, 1969.

Chadwick, H. Munro. *Studies on Anglo-Saxon Institutions.* New York: Russell & Russell, Inc., 1963.

Checkland, S.G. *The Gladstones, A Family Biography.* Cambridge: The University Press, 1971.

Churchill, Winston S. *The Birth of Britain.* Vol. I of *A History of the English Speaking Peoples.* New York: Dodd, Mead & Company, 1956.

_____. *The Gathering Storm.* Vol. I of *The Second World War.* Boston: Houghton Mifflin, 1948.

Clark, Cecily (ed.). *The Peterborough Chronicle: 1070-1154.* Oxford English Monographs. Edited by J.R.R. Tolkien, F.P. Wilson, and Helen Gardner. Oxford: The University Press, 1958.

Corbett, William John. *Germany and the Western Empire.* Vol. III of *The Cambridge Medieval History.* Edited by H.M. Gwatkin *et al.* Cambridge: The University Press, 1957.

Craigie, W.A., "The Nationality of King Alfred's Wulfstan," *Journal of English and German Philology,* Vol. XXIV, 396-397.

Dolley, R.H.M. (ed.). *Anglo-Saxon Coins.* London: Methuen & Co., Ltd., 1961.

Donaghey, Brian S. "The Sources of King Alfred's Translation of Boethius *De Consolatione Philosophiae.*" *Anglia,* LXXXII (1964), pp. 23-57.

Duckett, Eleanor Shipley. *Alfred the Great.* Phoenix Books. Chicago: The University of Chicago Press, 1958.

Ekblom, R. "Alfred the Great as Geographer," *Studia Neophilologica,* XIII (1940/41), 115-144.

_____. "Ohthere's Voyage from Skiringssal to Hedeby," *Studia Neophilologica,* XII (1939/40), 177-190.

English Historical Documents c. 500-1042. Vol. I. Edited by Dorothy Whitelock. New York: Oxford University Press, 1955.

Fisher, E.A. *An Introduction to Anglo-Saxon Architecture and Sculpture.* New York: Frederick A. Praeger, 1959.

Freeman, Edward A. *The History of the Norman Conquest of*
England, Its Causes and Its Results. Vol. I. Oxford: The
Clarendon Press for Macmillan and Co., New York,
1873.

Gatch, Milton McC. *Loyalties and Traditions: Man and His
World in Old English Literature.* New York: Pegasus, a division of The Bobbs-Merrill Company, Inc., 1971.

"Geography." *Encyclopaedia Britannica,* 1965, X, 144-159.

Giles, J.A. (ed.). *The Whole Works of King Alfred the Great
with Preliminary Essays.* Vols. I & II. New York: AMS
Press, 1969. Reprinted from the 1858 ed., London.

_____. (ed.). *Memorials of King Alfred, Being Essays on the
History and Antiquities of England During the Ninth Century,
the Age of King Alfred.* New York: Burt Franklin, 1969.
Reprinted from the 1863 ed.

Gneuss, Helmut. "The Origin of Standard Old English and
Aethelwold's School at Winchester." *Anglo-Saxon England,*
Vol. I, Ed. Peter Clemoes. Cambridge: University Press,
1973.

Godfrey, Walter H. *The Story of Architecture in England.* Part
I, *From Roman Times to the Reformation.* Part II, *From Tu-
dor Times to the End of the Georgian Period.* London: B.T.
Batsford, Ltd., 1931.

Harmer, F.E., *Anglo-Saxon Writs,* Manchester: Manchester
University Press, 1952.

Harrison, Frederick. *The Writings of King Alfred.* New
York: Haskell House, 1966.

Harrison, Kenneth. "The Beginning of the Year in England, c. 500-900." *Anglo-Saxon England,* Vol. II. Ed. Peter
Clemoes. Cambridge: University Press, 1973.

Helm, P.J. *Alfred the Great.* New York: Thomas Y. Crowell
Company, 1963.

Herold, Curtis Paul. *The Morphology of King Alfred's Translation of the Orosius.* The Hague: Mouton, 1968.

Hitchcock, E.V. and Chambers, R.W. (eds.). *Nicholas Harpsfield's Life of Sir Thomas More.* London: Oxford University Press, 1932.

Hodgkin, R.H. *A History of the Anglo-Saxons.* Vol. II. 3rd
ed. London: Oxford University Press, 1952, reprinted
1959.

Holdsworth, Sir William. *A History of English Law.* Vol. I,
7th ed. revised, 1956. Edited by A.L. Goodhart and H.G.

Hanbury with an Introductory Essay and Additions by S.B. Chrimes. London: Methuen & Co., Ltd. and Sweet and Maxwell, 1966.

———. *A History of English Law.* Vol. II, 4th ed., 1936. London: Methuen & Co., Ltd. and Sweet and Maxwell, 1966.

Hubener, Gustav, "Koenig Alfred's Geografie." *Speculum,* VI (July 1931), pp. 428-34.

Hume, David. *The History of England from the Invasion of Julius Caesar to the Abdication of James the Second, 1688.* Vol. I. Philadelphia: Claxton, Remsen & Haffelfinger, 1800.

Ingram, John Kells. "Slavery." *Encyclopaedia Britannica,* 1965, XX, pp. 773-784.

Jackson, Kenneth, *et al. Celt and Saxon: Studies in the Early British Border.* Cambridge: The University Press, 1963.

Kendrick, T.D., *Anglo-Saxon Art to A.D. 900.* London: Methuen & Co. Ltd., 1972.

Ker, N.R. (ed.) *The Pastoral Care, Early English Manuscripts in Facsimile,* Vol. VI. Copenhagen: Rosenkilde and Bagger, 1956.

King Alfred's Anglo-Saxon Version of Boethius de Consolatione Philosophiae. With a Literal English Translation, Notes, and Glossary by the Reverend Samuel Fox. New York: AMS Press, 1970. Reprinted from the 1864 ed.

Kispert, Robert J. *Old English: An Introduction.* New York: Holt Rinehart and Winston, Inc., 1971.

The Laws of the Earliest English Kings. Edited and Translated by F.L. Attenborough. New York: Russell & Russell, Inc., 1963.

Leeds, E. Thurlow. *The Archaeology of the Anglo-Saxon Settlements.* Oxford: Clarendon Press, 1970. Reprinted from 1913 ed.

Lees, Beatrice Adelaide. *Alfred the Great: The Truth Teller, Maker of England 848-899.* New York: G.P.Putnam's Sons, 1915.

Levison, Wilhelm. *England and the Continent in the Eighth Century.* Oxford: The Clarendon Press, 1956. Reprinted from the 1946 ed.

Liebermann, F. *Die Gesetze der Angelsaehsen.* Vols. I, II & III, Aalen, Germany: Scientia, 1960. Reprinted from the 1903-16 ed.

Liggins, Elizabeth M. "The Authorship of the Old English *Orosius,*" *Anglia* LXXXVIII (1970), pp. 289-322.

Lovell, Colin Rhys. *English Constitutional and Legal History:* *A Survey.* New York: Oxford University Press, 1962.

Loyn, H.R. *Anglo-Saxon England and the Norman Conquest.* A vol. of *Social and Economic History of England* edited by Asa Briggs. New York: St. Martin's Press, 1962.

Mackinnon, Albert G. *The Rome of the Medieval Church* (Earlier Section). London: The Butterworth Press, 1935.

Malone, Kemp. "The Old English Period." *A Literary History of England.* Edited by Albert C. Baugh. New York: Appleton-Century-Crofts, Inc., 1948.

_____. "King Alfred's North: A Study in Mediaeval Geography," *Speculum* V (1930), pp. 139-167.

_____. "On King Alfred's Geographical Treatise," *Speculum* VIII, pp. 67-78.

Mapp, Alf J., Jr. *The Virginia Experiment: The Old Dominion's Role in the Making of America* (1607-1781). Richmond: The Dietz Press, Inc., 1957.

Moore, Samuel and Thomas A. Knott. *The Elements of Old English* . 10th ed. revised. Ann Arbor, Michigan: The George Wahr Publishing Co., 1955.

Pauli, R. *The Life of Alfred the Great.* Translated by B. Thorpe. London: George Bell & Sons, 1902.

Myres, J.N.L. *Anglo-Saxon Pottery and the Settlement of England.* Oxford: Clarendon Press, 1969.

Page, R.I. *Life in Anglo-Saxon England.* New York: G.P. Putnam's Sons, 1970.

Payne, F. Anne. *King Alfred & Boethius: An Analysis of the Old English Version of the Consolation of Philosophy.* Madison: The University of Wisconsin Press, 1968.

Plucknett, Theodore F.T. *A Concise History of the Common Law.* 5th ed. London: Butterworth & Co., Ltd., 1956.

Plummer, Charles. *The Life and Times of Alfred the Great: Being the Ford Lectures for 1901.* Oxford: The Clarendon Press, 1902.

Plummer, Charles and John Earle. *Two of the Saxon Chronicles: Parallel with Supplementary Extracts from the Others.* 2 vols. Oxford: The Clarendon Press, 1965. Reprinted from the 1899 ed.

Pollock, Sir Frederick and Frederick William Maitland. *The History of English Law Before the Time of Edward I.* Vol. I, 2nd ed. Cambridge: University Press, 1899.

Potter, Simeon. "Commentary on King Alfred's Orosius," *Anglia,* LXXI (1953), pp. 385-437.

Robbins, Alfred F. "Ancestry and Early Life." Vol. I of *The Life of William Ewart Gladstone.* Edited by Sir Wemyss Reid. New York: Putnam, 1899.

Robinson, F.N. (ed.). *The Works of Geoffrey Chaucer.* 2nd ed. Boston: Houghton Mifflin Company, 1957.

Schilling, Hugo. *König Aelfred's Angelsachsiche Bearbeitung der Weltgeschichte des Orosius.* Halle-Max Niemeyer, 1886.

Schmidt, Albert F. *The Yeoman in Tudor and Stuart England.* Washington: The Folger Library, 1961.

Sedgefield, Walter John (ed.). *King Alfred's Old English Version of Boethius de Consolatione Philosophiae.* Oxford: Clarendon Press, 1899.

Stenton, F.M. *Anglo-Saxon England.* 2nd ed. Oxford: The Clarendon Press, 1955. Reprinted from 1947 ed.

_____. *Anglo-Saxon England.* 3rd ed. Oxford: The Clarendon Press, 1971.

Sweet's Anglo-Saxon Primer. 9th ed. revised by Norman Davis. Oxford: The Clarendon Press, 1953 with corrections 1957.

Sweet, Henry (ed.). *King Alfred's Orosius.* Part I. Published for The Early English Text Society. London: Oxford University Press, 1959. Reprinted from the 1883 ed.

_____. (ed.). *King Alfred's West Saxon Version of Gregory's Pastoral Care.* London: Oxford University Press, 1872.

Taylor, H.M. and Joan Taylor. *Anglo-Saxon Architecture.* 2 vols. Cambridge: The University Press, 1965.

Toynbee, Arnold J. *A Study of History.* New York: Oxford University Press, 1947.

Ullman, Walter. *The Growth of Papal Government in the Middle Ages: A Study in the Ideological Relation of Clerical to Lay Power.* 2nd ed. New York: Barnes & Noble, Inc., 1962.

Vico, Giambattista. *The New Science of Giambattista Vico.* Revised Translation of the Third Edition (1744) by Thomas Goddard Bergin and Max Harold Fisch. Ithaca, New York: Cornell University Press, 1968.

Wainwright, F.T. "Aethelflaed Lady of the Mercians." *The Anglo-Saxons.* Edited by Peter Clemoes. London: Bowes & Bowes, 1959.

Watson, Annah Robinson. *A Royal Lineage: Alfred the Great: 901-1901.* Richmond, Virginia: Whittet & Shepperson, 1901.

Weintraub, Karl J. *Visions of Culture*. Chicago: University of Chicago Press, 1966.

West, Stanley. "Archaeology 2390: A Saxon Village in East Anglia," *The Illustrated London News*. (February 1974), pp. 53-54.

Whitelock, Dorothy. *The Beginnings of English Society*. Aylesbury: Penguin Books, 1956.

———. *Changing Currents in Anglo-Saxon Studies*. Cambridge: University Press, 1958.

Wilson, D.M. *The Anglo-Saxons*. New York: Frederick A. Praeger, 1962.

Wulfing, J. Ernst. *Die Syntax in den Werken Alfreds des Grossen*, Vol. I, 1894; Vol. II, 1897. Bonn: P. Hanstein's Verlag, 1894-1897.

Yale Studies in English. Vol. XXII, *King Alfred's Old English Version of St. Augustine's Soliloquies Turned into Modern English by Henry Lee Hargrove*. Edited by Albert S. Cook. (New York, 1904).

Zesmer, David M. *Guide to English Literature from Beowulf Through Chaucer and Medieval Drama*. New York: Barnes & Noble, Inc., 1963.

END NOTES

[1]Though the designation "Alfred the Great" was not much used until the seventeenth century publication of Sir John Spelman's biography, and not truly popularized before the work's republication in 1709 as *The Life of Alfred the Great*, references to Alfred as the greatest of England's rulers had been multiplying since the ninth century.

[2]The Welsh bishop (d. *c.* 909) who was Alfred's friend, teacher, and first biographer.

[3]J. A. Giles, *Memorials of King Alfred* (New York: Burt Franklin, 1863 rpr. 1969), p. 128. Ethelweard, descended from Alfred's brother Ethelred, was the author of a chronicle of England. The chronicles of Ethelweard, Florence of Worcester, Henry of Huntingdon, are printed in parallel columns in this volume.

[4]Ibid.

[5]Ibid.

[6]P. J. Helm, *Alfred the Great* (New York: Thomas Y. Crowell Co., 1963), p. 192.

[7]R. Pauli, *The Life of Alfred the Great*, trans. B. Thorpe (London: George Bell & Sons, 1902), p. 116. Quoted from Gibbon's *Outlines of the History of the World—Miscellaneous Works* III, 3rd ed., 1814.

[8]David Hume, *The History of England from the Invasion of Julius Caesar to the Abdication of James the Second*, Vol. I (Philadelphia: Claxton, Remsen & Haffelfinger [1800]), p. 69.

[9]Karl J. Weintraub, *Visions of Culture* (Chicago: University of Chicago Press, 1966), p. 58.

[10]Ibid., p. 49.

[11]Eleanor Shipley Duckett, *Alfred the Great* (Phoenix Books; Chicago: The University of Chicago Press, 1958), pp. vii-viii.

[12]Edward A. Freeman, *The History of the Norman Conquest of England*, Vol. I (Oxford: Clarendon Press for Macmillan and Co., New York, 1873), p. 33.

[13]R. H. Hodgkin, *A History of the Anglo-Saxons*, Vol, II (3rd ed.; London: Oxford University Press, 1952 repr. 1959), p. 673.

[14]Winston S. Churchill, *A History of the English-speaking Peoples*, Vol. I *The Birth of Britain* (New York: Dodd, Mead & Company, 1956), pp. 126-127.

[15]William John Corbett in *Germany and the Western Empire,
The Cambridge Medieval History*, ed. H. M. Gwatkin et al,
Vol. III (Cambridge: The University Press, 1957), 352.

Chapter II

[1]Re Charlemagne's beard, see Charles Edward Russell,
Charlemagne (Boston: Houghton Mifflin Co., 1930), p. 251.

[2]Giambattista Vico. *The New Science of Giambattista Vico*,
trans. Thomas Goddard Bergin and Max Harold Fisch (3rd
ed.; Ithaca, New York: Cornell University Press, 1968), pp.
135-136.

[3]*The Anglo-Saxon Chronicle*, ed. Dorothy Whitelock *et al*
(New Brunswick, New Jersey: Rutgers University Press,
1961), p. 35.

R. H. Hodgkin, *A History of the Anglo-Saxons*, Vol. II (3rd
ed.; London: Oxford University Press, 1952, repr. 1959), p.
473.

The date is sometimes given as 789. For an explanation
of discrepancies in Anglo-Saxon chronology and matters of
related interest, see Miss Whitelock's excellent introduction,
The Anglo-Saxon Chronicle, pp. xi-xxix.

[4]*Anglo-Saxon Chronicle*, p. 36.

[5]Hodgkin, II, p. 474.

[6]*Anglo-Saxon Chronicle*, pp. 36-37.

[7]The modern term "earl" is used here as an approxima-
tion of the Old English "ealdorman," or "chief man," which
seems to have been supplanted by "earl" in the first half of
the eleventh century. See H. Munro Chadwick, *Studies on
Anglo-Saxon Institutions* (New York: Russell & Russell, Inc.,
1963), pp. 161-165.

[8]*Anglo-Saxon Chronicle*, p. 41.

[9]Ibid., p. 42.

[10]Hodgkin, II, pp. 473-509.

D. M. Wilson, *The Anglo-Saxons* (New York: Frederick
A. Praeger, 1962), pp. 93, 104-131.

[11]Helm, p. 48.

[12]F. M. Stenton, *Anglo-Saxon England* (2nd ed.; Oxford:
The Clarendon Press, 1947, repr. 1950, 1955), pp. 230-231.

[13]*Anglo-Saxon Chronicle*, p. 40, n. 7.

[14]Ibid., p. 40.

[15]Ibid., p. 41.

[16]Ibid.
[17]Ibid., p. 42.
[18]Ibid., pp. 58, 206-207.
Asser's Life of King Alfred, ed. William Henry Stevenson (Oxford: The Clarendon Press, 1959), pp. 1, 152-153.
[19]*Anglo-Saxon Chronicle*, p. 42.
[20]J. A. Giles (ed.), *The Whole Works of King Alfred the Great: with Preliminary Essays*, Vol. I (New York: AMS Press, 1969), p. 12. This translation is given here as perhaps more evocative of the flavor of the original, though not so esthetically pleasing as Dorothy Whitelock's in the *Anglo-Saxon Chronicle*, p. 42.
[21]*Anglo-Saxon Chronicle*, p. 43.
[22]Ibid.

Chapter III

[1]For example, dragon designs on the Gandersheim casket, Brunswick, Ducal Museum, as reproduced in D. M. Wilson, *The Anglo-Saxons*, p. 67
[2]Giles, *The Whole Works*, Vol. I, p. 329.
Beatrice Adelaide Lees, *Alfred the Great: The Truth Teller, Maker of England 848-899*. (New York: G. P. Putnam's Sons, 1915), p. 305.
The schedule of the court's peripatetic progress is from Helm, p. 57, and the descriptions of living conditions, transportation, dress, etc., are based largely on D. M. Wilson, *The Anglo-Saxons*.
[3]Helm, p. 34.
[4]Dorothy Whitelock (ed.), *English Historical Documents c. 500-1042*, Vol. I; general editor of *English Historical Documents* is David C. Douglas (New York: Oxford University Press, 1955), p. 266.
[5]Helm, p. 33.
[6]Ibid., pp. 29-30.
[7]*nobilis ingenio, nobilis et genere*, Asser, p. 4.
[8]*religiosa nimium femina*, Ibid.
[9]Wilson, pp. 104-131.
[10]Helm, pp. 35, 39.
[11]H. M. Taylor and Joan Taylor, *Anglo-Saxon Architecture*, Vols. I and II (Cambridge: The University Press, 1965).
Walter H. Godfrey, *The Story of Architecture in England*

(London: B. T. Batsford, Ltd., 1931), Part I, pp. 17-29.

E. A. Fisher, *An Introduction to Anglo-Saxon Architecture and Sculpture* (New York: Frederick A. Praeger, 1959), pp. 21-60.

[12]The picture of Rome at the time of Alfred's visit is based on Albert G. Mackinnon, *The Rome of the Medieval Church* London: The Butterworth Press, 1935.

[13]The discussion of Leo IV is based largely on Walter Ullman, *The Growth of Papal Government in the Middle Ages* (2nd. ed.; New York: Barnes & Noble, Inc., 1962), pp. 159-160, 174-176.

[14]*de omnibus quae in mundo sunt*, ibid., p. 175.

[15]Ibid. The exact significance of the ceremony to Leo IV seems to have been generally overlooked by Alfred's biographers.

[16]*Anglo-Saxon Chronicle*, p. 43.

[17]Asser, p. 20, where the dialogue is reproduced in Latin.

[18]As in the famous "Riddle of the Book."

[19]Asser, p. 19.

[20]The Vivian Bible (Bibl. Nat., Lat. I, f. 423^a. Paris) has an illustration (reproduced in Hodgkin, Vol. II, plate 67) of Charles II enthroned, with Count Vivian, lay abbot of Tours (843-851), standing at his side.

[21]Mackinnon, pp. 218-220.

[22]Helm, pp. 38-39.

[23]Duckett, p. 35.

[24]Asser, pp. 11-12.

[25]Einard modified. See Russell, pp. 251-252.

[26]Asser, pp. 13-14.

[27]Ibid., p. 9.

[28]Ibid., p. 10.

[29]Ibid.

[30]Duckett, p. 49.

[31]Adapted from the now classic translation by Charles W. Kennedy, published by Oxford University Press. The Kennedy version, backed by great erudition, is the most satisfying one in publication, and considerable audacity is required for us to substitute "earthly" for Kennedy's "worldly," but the connotation of the former seems to us more appropriate in this context.

[32]*Anglo-Saxon Chronicle*, p. 44.

[33]The Will of King Alfred, *English Historical Documents*, p. 492. See also appendix of *The Golden Dragon*.

[34]Ibid.

[35]Asser, p. 32.

[1]Hodgkin, Vol. II, p. 503.
[2]Lees, p. 108.
[3]Hodgkin, Vol. II, pp. 530-531.
  Stenton, pp. 244-246.
  Anglo-Saxon Chronicle, p. 45.
[4]Duckett, p. 47.
  Lees, pp. 107-108.
  Hodgkin, Vol. II, p. 526.
[5]Stenton, pp. 88-95.
[6]Hodgkin, Vol. II, p. 524.
  Anglo-Saxon Chronicle, p. 45.
[7]Hodgkin, Vol. II, p. 530.
[8]*Anglo-Saxon Chronicle*, p. 46.
  Asser, pp. 24-25.
[9]Asser, pp. 23-24, 54-55.
[10]The "portrait" coins of Alfred, almost without exception, show him clean-shaven, R. H. M. Dolley, *Anglo-Saxon Coins* (London: Methuen & Co., Ltd., 1961), pp. 77-94, plates IX and X.
[11]Asser, pp. 54-55.
[12]...ita ut ne unius quidem horae securitatem habeat, qua aut illam infirmitatem non susineat aut sub illinus formidine lugubriter *prope* constitutus non desperet. Ibid., p. 76.
[13]Ibid., p. 55.
[14]Stenton, p. 246.
  Hodgkin, Vol. II, pp. 531-533.
[15]Hodgkin, Vol, II, p. 534.
[16]The description of the Battle of Ashdown is based on the following sources:
  Anglo-Saxon Chronicle, pp. 46-47.
  Asser, pp. 28-31.
  Hodgkin, Vol. II., pp. 543-548.
[17]Asser, p. 29.
[18]Ibid.

Chapter V

[1]Asser wrote that he himself had seen the lone thorn tree years later, still standing.
  Asser, p. 30.

205

[2]*Anglo-Saxon Chronicle*, p. 47.

Hodgkin, p. 548.

[3]Ibid.

[4]Colin Rhys Lovell, *English Constitutional and Legal History: A Survey* (New York: Oxford University Press, 1962), p. 16

Chadwick, p. 226.

[5]Lovell, p. 11.

Stenton, pp. 543-544.

For a different interpretation, see Chadwick, pp. 357-366.

[6]*English Historical Documents*, p. 493.

The subsequent account is derived from Alfred's will as reproduced in *English Historical Documents*, pp. 492-495.

[7]Stenton, p. 287.

[8]Wilson, pp. 108-110.

[9]*Anglo-Saxon Chronicle*, p. 47.

[10]"Eodem quoque anno Saxones cum iisdem paganis, ea condicione, ut ab eis discederent, pacem pepigerunt; quod et impleverunt."

Asser, p. 34.

[11]Hodgkin, Vol. II, p. 551.

Stenton, p. 248.

For discussion of the theory that these coins were minted at a later date on orders of another Halfdene, see Dolley, p. 80.

[12]Lovell, pp. 11-13.

[13]*The Laws of the Earliest English Kings*, edited and translated by F. L. Attenborough (New York: Russell & Russell, Inc., 1963), pp. 42-47.

[14]Helm, p. 112.

[15]Stenton, pp. 275, 300.

[16]Ibid., p. 276.

[17]Albert F. Schmidt, *The Yeoman in Tudor and Stuart England* (Washington: The Folger Shakespeare Library, 1961), p. 2.

[18]John Kells Ingram, "Slavery," *Encyclopaedia Britannica*, 1965, XX, p. 773.

[19]Lovell, pp. 21-22.

[20]Ibid, p. 24.

[21]Adapted from Samuel Fox's translation of Alfred's *Boethius*. Both the Anglo-Saxon original and Fox's translation are available in *King Alfred's Anglo-Saxon Version of Boethius de Consolatione Philosophiae*, trans. The Rev. Samuel Fox (New York: AMS Press, 1970), pp. 58-61.

[22]Adapted from Henry Sweet's translation of Alfred's preface to Gregory's *Pastoral Care.*

Sweet, Part I.

[23]D. M. Wilson, pp. 108-110.

[24]*Ibid*, pp. 115-119.

[25]Fox, pp. 58-61.

[26]Helm, p. 82.

[27]*Anglo-Saxon Chronicle*, p. 48.

Helm, p. 83.

[28]*Anglo-Saxon Chronicle*, p. 48.

[29]Ibid.

[30]Ibid.

[31]Ibid.

Chapter VI

[1]Asser, p. 76.

[2]*Anglo-Saxon Chronicle*, p. 49.

Asser, pp. 40-41.

[3]*Anglo-Saxon Chronicle*, p. 49.

[4]Ibid.

[5]Ibid.

[6]Asser, p. 41.

[7]Ensuing descriptions of Athelney in different seasons and under varying conditions of weather are based on facts presented by Peter J. Helm in *Alfred The Great*, p. 92, and by Beatrice Lees in *Alfred the Great: The Truth Teller*, p. 162, together with the nineteenth century illustration opposite which must show the isle little different from the way it appeared in Alfred's time. Mr. Helm's observations derive special value from the fact that Athelney has been his home.

[8]Asser, pp. 20, 59.

[9]Helm, p. 180.

Duckett, p. 75.

[10]Lees, pp. 435-437.

[11]*Boethius*, chapter XXVII, p. 95.

[12]Ibid., chapter XXX, p. 109.

[13]J. Q. Adams, *A Life of William Shakespeare* (Boston: Houghton Mifflin Co., 1923), p. 16. Adams says: "For it is now virtually certain that through a younger branch he was descended, as the poet maintained, from the noble family

of Arden of Park Hall, who proudly traced their line back to the Sheriff Ailwin, Great Guy of Warwick, the Saxon King Athelstan, and Alfred the Great." He adds (n. 2) that "Mrs. C. C. Stopes has effectively presented the right of the poet to his pedigree, in her *Shakespeare's Environment*, 1914, and *Shakespeare's Family*, 1901."

[14]*Boethius*, chapter XXI, p. 73.
[15]Ibid., chapter XXX, p. 111.
[16]*Anglo-Saxon Chronicle*, p. 49.

Chapter VII

[1]"...visoque rege, sicut dignum erat, quasi redivivum post tantas tribulationes recipientes, immenso repleti sunt gaudio, et ibi castra metati sunt una nocte." Asser, p. 45.
[2]Kennedy translation of *Beowulf*, ll. 1329-1332.
[3]Ibid., ll. 1325-1326.
[4]Ibid., ll. 1354-1356.
[5]*Anglo-Saxon Chronicle*, p. 49.
[6]The appearance of the church is reconstructed from Walter H. Godfrey, *The Story of Architecture in England*, Part I (London: B. T. Batsford, Ltd., 1931), pp. 23-27.
[7]Asser, pp. 46-47.
[8]*Anglo-Saxon Chronicle*, p. 50.
[9]Helm, pp. 81-82.

Chapter VIII

[1]Winston S. Churchill, *The Second World War*, Vol. I, *The Gathering Storm* (Boston: Houghton Mifflin Company, 1948), p. viii.
[2]Hodgkin, Vol. II, p. 575.
[3]Ibid., pp. 575-576.
[4]*Anglo-Saxon Chronicle*, p. 50.
[5]Hodgkin, Vol. II, pp. 593-596.
[6]Ibid., pp. 583-585.
[7]Stenton, p. 261.
[8]Hodgkin, Vol. II, pp. 585-590.
[9]*Anglo-Saxon Chronicle*, p. 51.
Stenton, p. 255.
[10]*Anglo-Saxon Chronicle*, p. 51.
[11]Eodem anno Alfred, Angulsaxonum rex, post incendia

urbium stragesque populorum, Lundoniam civitatem hon- END NOTES
orifice restauravit et habitabidem fecit....
Asser, p. 83.
[12]*Anglo-Saxon Chronicle*, p. 52.
[13]For difference between Rex Anglorum and Rex Angliae, see Lovell, *English Constitutional and Legal History*, 1962, pp. 10-11.
[14]Hodgkin, Vol. II, pp. 577-578.
[15]The date of this treaty is not certain (Attenborough, *The Laws*, p. 96). The text of the agreement appears in Attenborough, pp. 99-101. Helpful discussions of the document are in Hodgkin, Vol. II, pp. 577-581, and Stenton, pp. 257-258.
[16]*Anglo-Saxon Chronicle*, p. 53.
[17]Hodgkin, Vol. II, pp. 597-598.

Chapter IX

[1]Milton McC. Gatch, *Loyalties and Traditions: Man and His World in Old English Literature* (New York: Pegasus, a division of The Bobbs-Merrill Company, inc., 1971), p. 17.
[2]Alfred used the Anglo-Saxon word "speda," which may mean either "wealth" or "skill." This ambiguity is pointed out in Lees, p. 272.
[3]Asser, p. 59.
[4]Ibid., pp. 93-94.
[5]Ibid., pp. 71, 77, 329-30.
[6]Fisher.
Taylor and Taylor.
[7]Fisher, p. 28.
[8]Taylor and Taylor, Vols. I and II, especially Vol. I, 1-15.
[9]Fisher, p. 22.
[10]Ibid.
[11]*"Aedificiis aureis et argenteis,"* Asser, p. 77.
[12]Asser, pp. 329-330.
[13]Ibid., p. 59.
[14]Duckett, p. 105.
[15]T. D. Kendrick, *Anglo-Saxon Art to A.D. 900* (London: Methuen & Co. Ltd., 1972), pp. 216-222.
[16]Adapted from translation in Giles, *The Whole Works*, p. 87. Original in Asser, p. 59.
[17]Asser, pp. 90-91.

Chapter X

[1]Asser, p. 67.

[2]Whitelock, *English Historical Documents*, Vol. I, pp. 814-817.

[3]Asser, pp. 81-84.

Some have questioned that Alfred's scholar John and John, abbot of Athelney, were the same person. But the most skeptical analysis leaves a presumption of "strong possibility." See Janet M. Bately, "Grimbald of St. Bertin's" *Medium AEvum*, XXXV (1966), p. 2.

[4]Asser, pp. 63-66.

The English translation that follows is based largely on Giles, *Memorials of King Alfred*, pp. 90, 92, 94.

[5]Asser, pp. 73-75.

Giles, pp. 98, 100.

[6]Sweet (ed.), *King Alfred's Orosius*, Part I, pp. 2-8.

[7]Ibid.

[8]Giles, *Whole Works*, Vol. I, pp. 327-335.

T. D. Kendrick, *Anglo-Saxon Art to A. D. 800* (London: Methuen & Co., Ltd., 1972), p. 216.

[9]Sweet (ed.), *King Alfred's Orosius*, Part I, pp. 2-8.

[10]Ibid., p. xli.

[11]William H. Brown, Jr., *A Syntax of King Alfred's Pastoral Care* (The Hague: Mouton, 1970), p. 19.

[12]Cited in Brown, pp. 70-80.

[13]Henry Sweet (ed.), *King Alfred's West Saxon Version of Gregory's Pastoral Care* (London: Oxford University Press, 1872), pp. 34-35.

[14]Ibid., p. 38 (translation adapted from Sweet with reference also to facsimile of ms., N. R. Ker (ed.), *The Pastoral Care* Vol. VI of *Early English Manuscripts in Facsimile*, ed. Bertram Colgrave *et al* (Copenhagen: Resenkilde and Bagger, 1953).

[15]Ibid., p. 41.

[16]Ibid., p. 141.

[17]Ibid., p. 165.

[18]Giles, *Whole Works*, Vol. II, p. 10.

[19]Curtis Paul Herold, *The Morphology of King Alfred's Translation of Orosius* (The Hague: Mouton, 1968), p. 18.

Alfred's authorship of the English *Orosius*, confidently asserted by William of Malmesbury, and confidently reasserted by such prestigious Anglo-Saxon scholars as Sir Frank Stenton, Eleanor Shipley Duckett, and Dorothy Whitelock, has occasionally been challenged, notably in recent years by Elizabeth M. Liggins (*Anglia*, LXXXVIII, 289-322) and Janet M. Bately (*Anglia*, LXXXVIII, 433-459). On the other hand, R. H. C. Davis, after publication of Liggins' and Bately's theories, was still so convinced of Alfred's authorship of the Orosius that he cited similarities of style between passages in that work and the *Anglo-Saxon Chronicle* to renew the old claim that Alfred was one of the authors of the *Chronicle* (*History*, LVI, 169-182). Liggins specifically takes no issue with the contention that the English *Orosius* reflects "the King's special interests and sympathies" and considers it "perfectly possible" that some of the insertions were "composed by him." Bately, as an argument against Alfred's authorship, cites the frequent use of *Ladteow* as a translation of consul in the *Orosius* rather than *heretoga*, a choice favored by Alfred in works known to be written by him. She points out that "the sole example of the word *heretoga* to occur in the *Orosius* in any context appears in the list of contents." To us, this fact suggests an argument for Alfred's direction and editing inasmuch as the "contents" outline a drastic recasting of the Latin work.

[20]Stenton, *Anglo-Saxon England*, p. 271.

R. Ekblom, concluding in 1941 a detailed survey of the orientation of Alfred's geographical work ("Alfred the Great as Geographer," *Studia Neophilologica*, Uppsala, Lundequistska Bokhandein, 1941, Vol. XIII, pp. 115-144), observed that "most of Alfred's many data about direction are strikingly correct.... Centuries passed before the goegraphy of Northern and Central Europe was again treated with Alfred's care and clarity. It is amazing that as early as the end of the ninth century there should have been achieved a work like King Alfred's excursus in the translation of Orosius' History of the World."

[21]*Encyclopaedia Britannica* (1965), Vol. X, p. 146.

[22]Giles, *Whole Works*, Vol. II, pp. 41-42, n. 44.

[23]Ibid., p. 54, n. 78.

On Wulfstan's ethnic origin, see: Ekblom, "Alfred the Great as Geographer," *Studia Neophilologica*, Vol. XIII, p. 115.

W. A. Craigie, "The Nationality of King Alfred's Wulfstan," *Journal of English and German Philology*, XXIV, pp. 396-397.

[24]Translation adapted from Giles, *Whole Works*, Vol. II, p. 55, and in subsequent passages, also from Sweet (ed.), King Alfred's *Orosius*, Part I.

[25]Ibid., pp. 55-56, n. 84.

[26]Translation adapted from Giles, *Whole Works*, Vol. II, pp. 54-55.

[27]Ibid., p. 54.

[28]Hodgkin, Vol. II, p. 644.

[29]Giles, *Whole Works*, Vol. II, pp. 16-17.

[30]R. Ekblom, "Ohthere's voyage from Skiringssal to Hedeby," *Studia Neophilologica*, Vol. XII, pp. 177-190.

[31]Kemp Malone, "The Old English Period," *A Literary History of England*, ed. Albert C. Baugh (New York: Appleton-Century-Crofts, Inc., 1948), p. 15.

[32]David M. Zesmer, *Guide to English Literature* (New York: Barnes & Noble, Inc., 1961), pp. 22.

[33]Giles, *Whole Works*, Vol. II, p. 200.

For a detailed discussion of syntactical points of similarity among works attributed to Alfred, see J. Ernst Wulfing, *Die Syntax in den Werken Alfreds des Grossen*, I-II, Bonn, 1894-1897 (e.g.I, pp. 2-44, 55-75, and II, pp. 172-176).

[34]*Anglo-Saxon Chronicle*, p. xxiii.

[35]Ibid., pp. xxiii, 43.

[36]Hodgkin, Vol. II, p. 624.

[37]In our own twentieth century, C. S. Lewis has made Boethius the basis of one of his most sophisticated arguments in *The Screwtape Letters*.

[38]Helm, p. 172.

[39]Adapted from the E. Thompson translation of King Alfred's *Bede* in Giles, *The Whole Works*, Vol. I, 249, with the help of the A. S. Cook and C. B. Tinker translation.

[40]F. N. Robinson, *The Works of Geoffrey Chaucer* (2d. ed.; Boston: Houghton Mifflin Company, 1957), p. 320.

[41]Ibid.

[42]Frederick Harrison, *The Writings of King Alfred* (New York: Haskell House, 1966).

[43]Ibid., pp. 20-21.

Walter John Sedgefield (ed.), *King Alfred's Old English Version of Boethius De Consolatione Philosophiae* Oxford: Clarendon Press, 1899), p. 5.

[44]Harrison, p. 21.

[45]Ibid.

[46]Ibid.

[47]Ibid., pp. 21-22.

[48]The dispute over authorship of the verses is well summarized by Kenneth Sissum, *Studies in the History of Old English Literature*, Oxford, 1962, pp. 292-297.

[49]Author of *King Aelfred's Angelsochsische Bearbeitung der Weltgeschicht des Orosius,* 1886.

[50]Plummer, p. 165.

[51]Ibid., pp. 180-181.

[52]Brian S. Doneghey, "The Sources of King Alfred's Translation of Boethius *De Consolatione Philosophiae,*" *Anglia,* LXXXII (1964), 23-57.

[53]Harrison, p. 24.

[54]*King Alfred's Boethius,* p. 187.

[55]Sedgefield, p. 75.

[56]Harrison, p. 26.

[57]Sedgefield, p. 174.

[58]Translated by the author with much help from Fox, *Boethius,* pp. 221-225.

[59]F. Anne Payne, *King Alfred & Boethius* (Madison: The University of Wisconsin Press, 1968), pp. 97-98.

[60]Donaghey, p. 59.

[61]Payne, pp. 90-91.

[62]Ibid., pp. 50-51.

[63]The reader seriously interested in pursuing this analogy might profitably read not only Miss Payne's book but also James' *The Will to Believe* and Tillich's *Systematic Theology.*

[64]Lees, p. 367.

[65]*Yale Studies in English,* Albert S. Cook, ed., XXII, *King Alfred's Old English Version of St. Augustine's Soliloquies Turned into Modern English by Henry Lee Hargrove.* (New York, 1904), pp. 1-2.

[66]Ibid.

[67]Ibid., p. 36.

[68]Ibid.

[69]Ibid.

[70]Ibid., p. 47.

[71]Malphe, p. 99.

[72]Ibid., pp. 104-105.

[73]Stenton, p. 272.

[74]Ibid.

Chapter XI

[1]Hodgkins, Vol. II, p. 606.

[2]Holdsworth, pp. 107-110.

[3]Sir Frederick Pollock and Frederick William Maitland, *The History of English Law Before the Time of Edward I*, Vol. I (2nd ed.; Cambridge: University Press, 1899), pp. 38-39.

[4]Theodore F. T. Plucknett, *A Concise History of the Common Law* (5th ed.; London: Butterworth & Co., Ltd., 1956), pp. 118-119.

[5]Pollock and Maitland, p. 31.

[6]Ibid., p. 49.

[7]Marcwardt and Rosier, p. 302.
Pollock and Maitland, p. 60.

[8]Ibid.

[9]Ibid., pp. 61-62.

[10]Helen Cam, *Law-Finders and Law-Makers in Medieval England* (New York: Barnes & Noble, Inc., 1962), p. 12.

[11]Attenborough, p. 3.

[12]Ibid., pp. 18-19.

[13]Ibid., pp. 24-25.

[14]F. Lieberman, *Die Gesetze der Angelsachsen*, Vol. III, Aalen, Germany, Scientia, p. 34. Lieberman examines the arguments of Stevenson, Draper, Lynn, Ramsay, Plummer, Pauli, and Freeman for other dates.

[15]Attenborough, p. 35.

[16]Alf J. Mapp, Jr., *The Virginia Experiment* (Richmond: Dietz Press, Inc., 1957), p. 19.

[17]All quotations from Alfred's laws, like "The Laws of Alfred" in the appendix of this volume, are from Attenborough's translation. A fully annotated text in Anglo-Saxon and German, most useful to the specialist, is in F. Liebermann, *Die Gesetze der Angelsachsen*, Vol. I, Aalen, Germany, Scientia, pp. 15-123.

[18]H. Munro Chadwick, *Studies on Anglo-Saxon Institutions* (New York: Russell & Russell, Inc., 1963), pp. 355-366.

[19]The significance of the terms earl and ealdorman is discussed in Chadwick, *Studies*, pp. 163-164.

Chapter XII

[1]The ensuing account of Alfred's last great war with the Danes is based primarily on the *Anglo-Saxon Chronicle*, pp. 53-58, and secondarily on Stenton, *Anglo-Saxon England*, pp. 260-265, and Hodgkin, Vol. II, 653-669. The maps in Hodgkin are particularly valuable.

[2]*Anglo-Saxon Chronicle*, p. 54.

³Hodgkin, Vol. II, p. 661.

⁴The charred prows of the burned Viking vessels were unearthed when railway construction workers were digging the foundations of South Benfleet station.

⁵*Anglo-Saxon Chronicle*, p. 57.

⁶Giles, *Memorial*, p. 125.

⁷*Anglo-Saxon Chronicle*, p. 57.

⁸Ibid.

⁹Ibid.

¹⁰Ibid., p. 58.

¹¹Lees, pp. 462-463.

¹²Plummer, p. 196.

¹³Asser, pp. 54-55, 57.

¹⁴Kenneth Harrison, "The Beginning of the Year in England, c. 500-900," *Anglo-Saxon England* II, pp. 66-69.

¹⁵*Anglo-Saxon Chronicle*, p. 58.

¹⁶Adapted from the concluding lines of Charles W. Kennedy's translation of *Beowulf*.

Chapter XIII

¹Quotations from King Alfred's Will, and the text of the will as reproduced in the appendix of this volume, are from Dorothy Whitelock (ed.), *English Historical Documents*, Vol. I. pp. 873-888.

²Sir Arthur Bryant, *Makers of England* (New York: Doubleday & Company, Inc., 1962), p. 105.

³McC. Gatch, p. 17.

⁴F. T. Wainwright, "Aethelflaed Lady of the Mercians," *The Anglo-Saxons*, ed. Peter Clemoes (London: Bowes & Bowes, 1959), pp. 53-69.

⁵Churchill, *A History of the English Speaking Peoples*, Vol. I, p. 131.

⁶E. V. Hitchcock and R. W. Chambers (eds.), *Nicholas Harpsfield's Life of Sir Thomas More* (London: Oxford University Press, 1932), p. lxi.

⁷Bryant, p. 122.

Stenton, p. 364.

⁸Churchill, *A History of the English Speaking Peoples*, Vol, I, p. 140.

⁹Ibid., p. 144.

¹⁰Hitchcock and Chambers, p. lxx.

¹¹Stenton, pp. 635-636.

[12]Sir Frank Stenton, quoted in Dorothy Whitelock, *Changing Currents in Anglo-Saxon Studies* (Cambridge: University Press, 1958), p. 24.

[13]Whitelock, *Changing Currents*, pp. 22-23.

[14]Fisher, p. 22.

[15]Whitelock, *Changing Currents*, p. 26.

[16]Ibid.

[17]Ibid.

[18]Hitchcock and Chambers, pp. lvi-clxxiv.

[19]Ibid., p. lxxvi.

[20]Ibid., p. lvi.

[21]Ibid., p. lxv.

[22]Ibid., pp. lvi-lvii.

[23]Adams, Shakespeare, p. 16.

[24]Alfred F. Robbins, "Ancestry and Early Life," *The Life of William Ewart Gladstone*, ed. Sir Wemyss Reid (New York: Putnam, 1899), Vol. I, p. 58.

S.G. Checkland, *The Gladstones, A Family Biography* (Cambridge: The University Press, 1971), p. 38.

[25]Annah Robinson Watson, *A Royal Lineage: Alfred the Great 901-1901* (Richmond: Whittet & Shepperson, 1901), pp. 24-57.

[26]Bryant, p. 15.

[27]Arnold J. Toynbee, *A Study of History* (New York: Oxford University Press, 1947), p. 122.

[28]Plummer, p. 105.

INDEX

GENEALOGY

The West Saxon royal house (a).

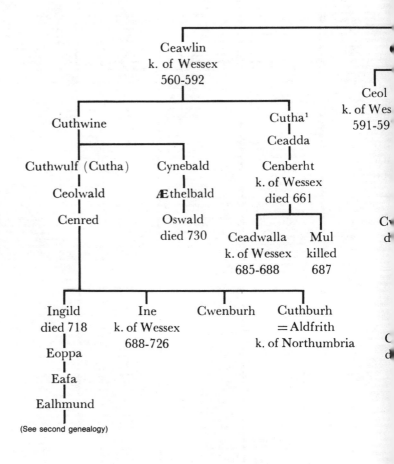

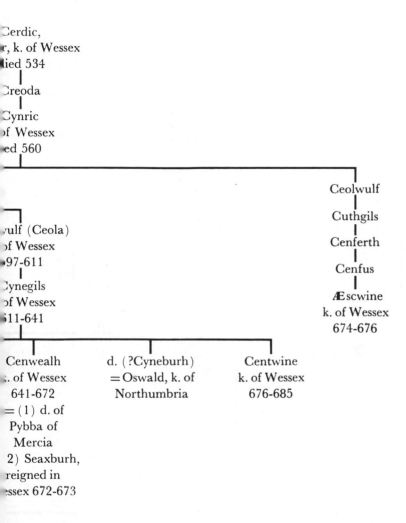

Cerdic,
r, k. of Wessex
died 534
|
Creoda
|
Cynric
of Wessex
ed 560
|
```
                                                                    Ceolwulf
                                                                       |
                                                                    Cuthgils
                                                                       |
   ulf (Ceola)                                                      Cenferth
   of Wessex                                                           |
   97-611                                                            Cenfus
      |                                                                |
   Cynegils                                                         Æscwine
   of Wessex                                                      k. of Wessex
   11-641                                                           674-676
```

Cenwealh	d. (?Cyneburh)	Centwine
. of Wessex	= Oswald, k. of	k. of Wessex
641-672	Northumbria	676-685
= (1) d. of		
Pybba of		
Mercia		
2) Seaxburh,		
reigned in		
essex 672-673		

'Cutha could however be a short form of Cuthwine.

hy Whitelock, ed., Eyre & Spottiswoode, Ltd.

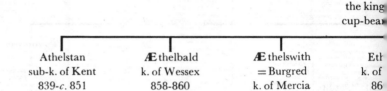

(1) Osb..
d. of Osl..
the king..
cup-bea..

Athelstan
sub-k. of Kent
839-*c*. 851

Æthelbald
k. of Wessex
858-860

Æthelswith
= Burgred
k. of Mercia

Eth
k. of
86

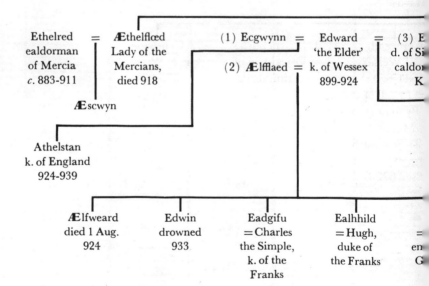

Ethelred
ealdorman
of Mercia
c. 883-911

=

Æthelflœd
Lady of the
Mercians,
died 918

(1) Ecgwynn

(2) Ælfflaed

=

=

Edward
'the Elder'
k. of Wessex
899-924

=

(3) E
d. of Si
caldo..
K

Æscwyn

Athelstan
k. of England
924-939

Ælfweard
died 1 Aug.
924

Edwin
drowned
933

Eadgifu
= Charles
the Simple,
k. of the
Franks

Ealhhild
= Hugh,
duke of
the Franks

=
en
G

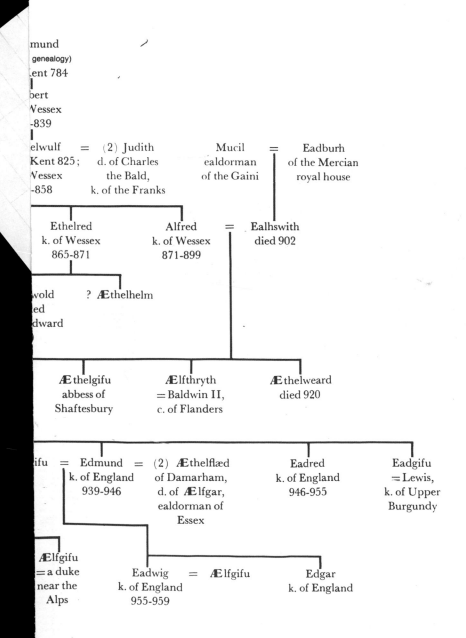

mund
(genealogy)
Kent 784
|
bert
Wessex
-839
|
elwulf   =   (2) Judith   Mucil   =   Eadburh
Kent 825;   d. of Charles   ealdorman   of the Mercian
Wessex   the Bald,   of the Gaini   royal house
-858   k. of the Franks

          Ethelred   Alfred   =   Ealhswith
          k. of Wessex   k. of Wessex   died 902
          865-871   871-899

wold   ? Æthelhelm
ed
dward

          Æthelgifu   Ælfthryth   Æthelweard
          abbess of   = Baldwin II,   died 920
          Shaftesbury   c. of Flanders

ifu   =   Edmund   =   (2) Æthelflæd   Eadred   Eadgifu
            k. of England   of Damarham,   k. of England   = Lewis,
            939-946   d. of Ælfgar,   946-955   k. of Upper
                              ealdorman of   Burgundy
                              Essex

Ælfgifu
= a duke
near the   Eadwig   =   Ælfgifu   Edgar
Alps   k. of England   k. of England
                   955-959

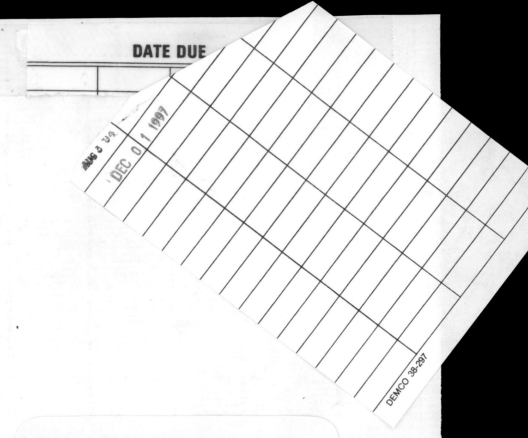